My Good Grief

To order additional copies, please contact us.
BookSurge, LLC
www.booksurge.com
1-866-308-6235
orders@booksurge.com

My Good Grief
A Journey through Joy and Sorrow

Cindyanne Kershaw

2006

To all those I love and have loved.

Chapter 1

"There is no way to happiness, happiness is the way"
Wayne Dyer

When I was growing up, my mother never told me about sorrow, not about real sorrow anyway. I wondered if she'd ever had any experience with it. When I was a little girl, I remember her having a fairly cheerful countenance. Of course, there were times when I sensed she wasn't happy with me, or with other things, yet she was never sorrowful that I can remember.

Somewhere in my memory banks though, there resides a feeling of sorrow from way back when I was a small child. I asked her about it once, explaining that two old songs, "April Showers" and "Oh How We Danced On The Night We Were Wed", always made me feel so sad that I wanted to cry. I can remember almost vividly, sitting at the bottom of the stairs one time with my doll in my arms, and feeling the tears well up in my eyes when I heard the music. I had no explanation for the feeling of sadness the memory evoked.

She told me that she couldn't remember anything particularly sad from that time when she used to play those two records which she'd always liked. She thought the whole thing might have been connected with my doll getting broken or something like that. In the back of my mind, that didn't ring true and with it came a fleeting memory of my mother crying, but I didn't persist in asking her something she had not divulged freely.

When I met up with my first experience of sorrow, I wasn't at all prepared for it. Would I have been if my mother had told me about it? I remember her mother dying at the age of 55. I was 17. To me my grandmother seemed old, so it didn't register as sorrowful to me. I don't remember my mother being that sad at the time either. I think she was glad to have her relatives around her, some who'd traveled some distance to come to the funeral. My memory pulls out happiness and laughter, rather than sorrow and tears.

How was I to know then that losing not just one, but two husbands to death would bring about such heart-wrenching sorrow. My mother never told me to expect such a thing would happen when I lost someone I loved.

What my mother never told me about sorrow, I learned from my first experience with losing my husband. I learned first hand about sorrow and its deep, piercing pain. When I married again, and several years later found my husband to be terminally ill, I was able to tell myself all about sorrow. It didn't help to know. It didn't make the losing of a beloved any easier.

What I know of sorrow is something I can tell you about now. I can tell you that one sorrow doesn't make another any easier. I can tell you that even if my mother had told me about real sorrow, I wouldn't have been prepared for the experiences of it that waited for me in my life. I can also tell you that when my younger brother drowned at the age of 32, my mother would have been able to tell me all about sorrow after that.

Maybe you haven't experienced heart-wrenching sorrow, maybe you have only experienced a little sorrow, or maybe you haven't experienced real sorrow in your life yet.

I want to write about mine to make a connection with you. I want to tell you about my sorrow, but more than telling you about my sorrow, I want to tell you about my joy.

If heart-wrenching sorrow and unbearable grief can devastate you, indescribable joy and unbelievable happiness can wipe it all away, balance everything out and bring you back again. Life has come back to surprise me so many times that I wonder why I'm always amazed when it happens. Seasons come and go and people come and go in our lives. Resolutely, we continue on, not knowing for sure what might be waiting for us around the next corner, yet as fragile as life seems at times, it still has the ability to come back stronger than ever and catch us by surprise.

When I'm reminded about joy, I'm reminded that life is a spectacular journey. Sometimes we forget about joy when times are hard. Sometimes life is fraught with so many obstacles, that we find it hard to remember how extraordinary it can be. Yet, ever so suddenly, it can change. Happiness is a bridge that spans the distance between sadness and sorrow. Joy and delight are the red blocks on the checkerboard between the black ones.

What a wonder it all is. Suddenly and seemingly without warning, life can come up all gold again. I take a morning swim in the lake where I live, on a lovely, summer day, and it dawns on me, as I'm showered with flakes of sunlight, that all is well. All is well with the world and with me. Life is precious and when I realize what an integral part of it I am, I am grateful. I am grateful for every experience, even the ones that were the most difficult to get through, grateful for the lessons I've learned, grateful to be alive.

❧

WILD GROWS MY GARDEN

Wild grows my garden,
something like me.
Profusion of color as far as you see.
Spread on my hillside, it laughs in the sun,
significantly sprawling, happy to be,
no boundaries, no borders, joyful and free.

Neat grew my garden,
controlled, just like me.
Curbed like my spirit, 'til you came to me.
Laid out on the hillside, blooms in the sun,
precise rows of color, no tangle of weeds.
No spirit, no laughter, empty of needs.

Your love, like my garden
demanded of me,
myself to acknowledge, as me you did see.
Wide did my arms spread, face to the sky,
All-encompassing life forces entered my heart,
undisciplined, boundless, with you at the start.

Wild grows my garden,
exactly like me,
wild with the ecstasy life's heaped on me.
Like the blooms on my hillside, I bask in your love.
Delight is abounding, for you've given me,
your heart and your soul, and with that set mine free.

Chapter 2

"Writing and reading decrease our sense of isolation.
They deepen and widen and expand our sense of life.
They feed the soul."
Anne Lamott, <u>Bird by Bird</u>

When I was 14 years old, I wanted to be a writer. Although discouraged in college by criticism I found hard to take at 18, I continued to write throughout my life. When I was 18, most of what I wrote was very personal, and the red slashes that covered the pages of my work were like whiplashes on my self-confidence. Writing remained a part of me anyway. For me it was never just a matter of wanting to; it was because I needed to. It fulfilled me. I felt the same need to write in happy times as in sad times, but during my grieving times, it became a solace. By putting my thoughts on paper when I felt the desolation of my grief, I was able to dispel some of the inner turmoil that was raging around inside of me.

Within the confines of my life, I have been married three times, divorced once, and widowed twice--all by my mid fifties. My second husband, David, died at 45, and my third husband, Walt, died at 51. During that time, I had also raised five children. The history of those years is recorded in notebooks and journals, and is included in hundreds of lines of poetry written for and about loved ones.

Writing is as much a part of me as breathing. Being able to express myself on paper is an integral part of my daily routine. I bring a spiral notebook with me wherever I go, in case the urge to write something comes over me. I enjoy transferring my thoughts onto a blank page. Inspiration often comes to me in my car; so nowadays when that happens, I record my thoughts into a small micro cassette recorder to save for future reference.

The beauty of the lake where I live surrounds me every season of the year. The atmosphere is very conducive to writing. In the morning, whenever the weather allows, I sit by the water with my pen, pad, and a cup of coffee. In the early evening, if the lake is calm, I often go out into the middle of it in my canoe, and sit there in the stillness, contemplating. Sometimes I write out there, too.

Although I write at the computer too, the act of taking pen to paper is much more satisfying to me than sitting and typing. Even though I write anywhere and everywhere, the best place is still by the water. There I can open up my heart and let go of all the emotions that swirl around inside of me. The water calms and quiets me and my thoughts.

What do I write about? I write about life, and how I feel about it. I write about myself and how I feel. I write about delight beyond measure, heart-wrenching sorrow, and all the laughter and tears in between. I write about everything on earth and under heaven. I think that covers it all.

Why do I write? I write because it always makes me feel better. It feeds my soul. Sometimes what I write for myself doesn't amount too much. When I read back over some of the things I've written, it often sounds redundant, wordy or trite to me, but on occasion, I read something I have written and find it so poignantly beautiful or profound, that I can hardly believe I wrote it.

I read somewhere that the process of talking and writing about your feelings toward others, improves your health, enhances immune function, and reduces cardiovascular reactivity. It is said that the greater the degree of disclosure, the more benefits came out of it. Since I disclose it all, I must have a very healthy heart and immune system!

When I'm writing because I'm happy, it feels like I'm spreading my wings. It feels like I'm soaring and gliding, opening up to the sky. When I'm sad and I write, it often feels like I'm expending my sorrows with every stroke of my pen, allowing myself to breath freer with every word. For me, writing is a therapy, a really good one.

BY THE WATER

Maybe you could come
and stand with me beside my lake.
With your arms wound tightly around me,
wedged together, standing there,
you'd know that it was good.

Maybe I could come
and be with you beside your sea.
With my hand held firmly in your hand,
hips just brushing, walking there,
I'd know that it was good.

Maybe we could go
and stand together by the falls.
With your fingers brushing back my hair,
I'd lift my face and find you there.
We'd know that it was good.

Maybe we could know
the peace that water always brings.
With our hearts and souls both open wide,
two bodies meeting, lying there,
we'd feel that it was good.

Chapter 3

"The only thing we have to fear is fear itself."
Franklin D. Roosevelt

Anyone who has ever been diagnosed with cancer, or has been close to someone who's received that diagnosis, can remember exactly where he or she was and what was going on at the time. The word itself throws fear into our hearts. The prospect of a loved one having cancer is the ultimate fear. When we first hear the verdict we're ready to accept it as a death sentence. That is the spontaneous reaction to the news. The reality of what having cancer means, all its properties, treatments, and cures, doesn't enter into our thinking at the very beginning. It isn't until the news has filtered through our brain, and our hearts have settled back into place, that we begin to think logically about it and grasp for hope.

The other day a close relative told me that her husband had lung cancer. A memory flooded over me so vividly that my heart lurched. I could smell the musky odor of the autumn leaves I had been raking on the day I had heard the news that my husband, David, had lung cancer. He was 40 years old, and suddenly life, formerly so full of promise, had become a darkened hallway with a closed door at the end. The air was close and it was hard to breathe. Life as I'd known it would never be the same again. A feeling of overwhelming loss enveloped me. I was already thinking about all the things that could never be and about events that would never happen. The word "cancer" had changed our lives in an instant. I grieved over my loss ahead of time, as if it had already happened.

I raked the leaves numbly that fall day, methodically, going over the recent scenario. My thoughts about so many mundane issues suddenly became of no consequence. My heart and my mind were tied in knots over the devastating news. I began to think about what to do next. Purpose gave me back my strength. A problem situation always brought out the best in me, as I shifted into high gear, organizing my thoughts, researching and coming up with practical solutions. Actively doing something helped take my mind off my emotional state.

Looking back on that time, over twenty years ago, I remember that I didn't get to a calm place right away. Almost blindly I went about the business of arranging for doctor's visits, chemotherapy, and later, radiation. David proceeded to go through various treatments for his lung cancer, and experienced the reactions to the therapies. We learned what dealing with cancer really meant.

Because I've always had a faith that resided within me, especially through the difficult times, I called on that faith, and actually became calmer and more peaceful in my acceptance of life as it was, not as I wished it to be. I read incessantly--first about cancer and cures, mainstream and alternative, and then about cures for sadness, cures for despair, and cures for hopelessness.

In the long run, the time of David's illness, which covered a period of five years, came to be a time when life seemed very worthwhile. Each day felt like a blessing. It's amazing how your perspective changes when you don't take each day for granted. Every new treatment brought hope, even when hope seemed almost too distant to reach for. As

I filled myself up with all kinds of inspiring writings and came face to face with how fragile life really was, I began to view it from a different perspective.

Every serious illness and every death touches us, and should. Each time we are reminded that we don't have forever to walk this earth. We are reminded not to put off until tomorrow what we really should be doing today. It brings us up short and asks us, "What is really important? What is really meaningful?" The answer usually comes down to the people we love and care about. When the prospect of death lingers around the edges of our lives, we become aware of how little time we carve out from our busy schedules to spend with those who mean the most to us.

The original fears stopped plaguing my mind when I began my acceptance of life's unfolding. I didn't know if my husband would die from this cancer. It was always my hope that even if his cancer couldn't be cured, he could still live many years. I decided that the most important thing was to remain optimistic and keep the fears under control.

I don't think that I would advocate grieving ahead of time. It might be a journey to a place that never even materializes, and that makes it a waste of precious time and energy. It also influences your mood and state of mind and keeps you in a place of sadness. It isn't easy to act like all is well when underneath the exterior you're aware that the roof could cave in at any time, but it's a much better choice. There's time enough to grieve when you lose a loved one. Besides, when a loved one has a serious illness, the person who becomes the caretaker is usually someone close to them, and it takes all their strength and fortitude, along with an optimistic countenance, to accomplish the task.

In the beginning, it seems only natural to be there for someone you love and so you take on the task gladly. If you ever knew ahead of time how difficult it could become as the illness progressed, you might never be able to start. Watching someone you love deteriorate is heartbreaking. It is almost impossible at times to remain positive.

To be a good caretaker, you have to also take good care of yourself. It is so necessary to take time off from the job as caretaker, and go off and forget the gloom that sometimes hovers around the place where the illness resides. When I took the time to go out and be with other people, I found it easier to bear the sorrow that sat beside me at home when I returned to my caretaker role once more.

When someone you love is terminally ill, being a caretaker for them is not any easy job, no matter how you choose to go about the task. I had to do it alone because that was the way it worked best for me. I couldn't stand to see my own pain reflected in someone else's eyes, or know that anyone felt sorry for me. It threatened to undermine my composure.

One time when I was deeply involved in my role as a caretaker, my youngest daughter came home for the weekend for a visit. We sat quietly together and she, knowing I was close to tears, put her arm around me. All the love she passed on to me with that gesture made me feel like I could easily let go, and just break apart into little pieces. I knew I couldn't allow that. I had to remain stable. I couldn't afford to let go even for a few moments. Comfort and sympathy were detrimental to my hard won stability in dealing with my own sadness at that point.

When I was a caretaker, I found my salvation in the outdoors, in Nature. It was always a respite for me during those difficult days. I'd drink in the view, whether it was a spectacular sunrise or sunset, the sun on the water on a warm summer afternoon, a gloriously colorful autumn day, or a winter landscape covered with a blanket of soft white snow. I'd wonder how it could remain so beautiful through every season. Then I'd feel like I couldn't possibly be sad in the face of all that magnificence. Observing such beauty, so simply stated, renewed me.

FEAR NO FEAR

I feel my fear.
Icy cold fingers of it grip my heart.
My soul is scathed with bands of it.
It seizes me unbidden.
I fall to my knees.
I pray.
I weep unceasingly.
My heart hurts.
No fear.
I need to remember to fear not.
I need to retrieve my heart from its grip,
Free my soul to soar once again.
They support me.
I walk.
I run.
I have always done that when I've been afraid.
It clears my head.
Yet I have always tried to run away from fear.
I turn and face it now.
Belligerently I stab holes in its substance.
It dissipates.
It has no substance.

All my life I've fought valiantly against it,
Overcome the sorrows that walk with it.
I do it again now because I haven't quite conquered it.
I still haven't learned to trust.
Everlasting arms pick me up
and carry me once again through this valley.
I am comforted, and I will fear no evil.

Chapter 4

"When you are joyous, look deep into
your heart and you shall find that it is
only that which has given you sorrow
that is giving you joy"
Kahlil Gibran, The Prophet

When I was a young girl, I had a special place where I
would go when I was feeling sad. It might have been because
of an argument I'd had with a friend or the fact that my
mother had yelled at me for something. My haven was a
low hanging branch on a majestic maple tree in our front
yard. I'd make my way up the tree to that sturdy branch
which hung out over the road, and then I'd sit there feeling
completely cut off from the rest of the world. I don't even
know if my mother ever knew I went and sat there. Perched
on my branch with my head against the tree's trunk, I was
oblivious of the rough bark under me.

I would sit there and sing until I wasn't sad any more.
Sometimes I even cried because it was alright to do
so up there. I can still see myself sitting there singing
"Somewhere Over The Rainbow." I was Dorothy in the
Wizard of Oz and I had traveled far away from my everyday
cares. Cars traveled under the place where I had settled
myself, never noticing me sitting above them. It gave me
a sense of power, sitting there alone, high above the world,
completely cut off from everyone else.

In later years when I could drive, I'd go to the seashore when I felt sad. I'd go to a place our family had gone in the summer for many of my growing up years. There I would walk the sandbars I'd loved since I was a child, and feel my smallness in proportion to the vastness of the Universe.

To this day I'm still able to center myself in that stretch of sand and sky. I go to that place where the sky meets the sound and the sound meets the sandbars. Every time I set foot on those sandbars and walk there, I meet myself again. If I've been sad, I usually go home feeling better. I also love to go there when I am happy and walk along the sandbars, breathing in the salt air. Often I go there when it's nearing day's end, and watch the sunset, its glorious colors filling the sky around me.

If my heart is filled with delight, it's a good place to spread my arms, run, laugh, and rejoice. When I'm feeling down, it's a comforting place to go. In the peacefulness of that place, I'm reminded of the co-existence of both these aspects of my life.

Sometimes when I am sad and feeling alone, my aloneness is starkly apparent to me. All by myself, walking in that place where time seems to stand still, I can capture some of the peacefulness that reminds me that I'm never really alone. It strengthens me to be walking there, and I find that in the process I am taken apart and put back together again, a little better than before.

At times I feel that I am vulnerable to every change in perspective that comes my way. Each change determines how I feel. I don't like to give in to sadness especially when it comes over me unbidden, but I know that experiencing sorrow is what makes joy and happiness so monumental in comparison. There is a balance between the two. So I continue to go to that timeless place I love, because it has

the ability to change my perspective as soon as I set foot
on the wet sand.

✿

I SEE YOU

I walk inside the molds I've left still outlined in the sand.
As I reverse my journey's path,
I feel the imprints of my feet
and in my steps I see you.

I scan the houses on the shore--just sketches on the
beach.
Their faces watch as time and tide
and lifetimes pass their gaze,
and looking out I see you.

The baby waves come rolling in to play upon the sand.
They leave behind their lacey edge
to decorate the sprawling flats,
and in their wake I see you.

A canopy of deepest blue is background for a waning
moon.
Its panorama fades and pales
where edges meet and oceans reach,
and in the moon I see you.

Before me, a majestic rock recalls your form against it.
I touch its warmth and feel you still
as if you were before me,
and filled with joy I see you.

The tide is changing as I walk, for years have passed before me.
I've journeyed through the ebb and flow,
brought safely through its passage,
and still, and still I see you.

Chapter 5

"Passage through the darkness of
doubts and crisis is essential to
growth in the process of faith."
John Powell, <u>Deeper than Tears</u>

One definition of the word "faith" is: confidence or
trust in a person or thing. To me, faith is an unshakable
belief in something larger than oneself, something that's
unexplainable and can't quite be defined. Faith is an
incredible force that has been known to visibly affect lives
by changing the negative into the positive. It has the power
to wipe away doubt and center thought in a place where
hope lives eternally.

When faith is securely stationed within you, nothing
seems to be impossible. It's the bearer of good things coming
your way even when the prospect of that happening seems
remote. It's a belief in the impossible being possible, the
unswerving knowledge that everything eventually works
out, despite the way it might look at the moment.

Faith is secured by remembering the times when
everything came together just like a plan. Together in
the company of hope, faith helps make the future appear
bright on the horizon. It flourishes amidst the weeds and
decay of life, the word itself bringing with it a satisfying
ring of truth. I know, for I have been in a place where I felt
tangled by the weeds and suffocated by the decay, fearing
never to break free. I know, because I managed to keep in

sight the much sought after prize of a beautiful garden, where everything was planted healthy and new, yearning to grow again, and it saved me.

The bare trees in the early spring look as if green finery will never adorn their branches again. But when you take a moment to look close, you see the tiny buds just waiting for the warmth of the sunshine to help them burst into baby green leaves. The seemingly impossible will occur. Why should it be any different for us? Laid bare in the winter of our sorrow, we can still bud and bloom again when spring comes.

When I was about 9 years old, I possessed a childlike faith. I believed that there was a God, and that He loved me. One night, a very large man, who was a friend of my parents, stepped out our front door directly onto my favorite cat. When my father picked up my broken cat in his arms, I listened to him in tears as he said, "I'm sorry Cindy, but the cat is badly hurt. We'll put her in the garage, and if she makes it through the night, it will be a miracle."

I'd been to Sunday school regularly and I remembered about miracles. I remembered that if you asked for one, prayed hard, and truly believed, then it might come true. I did, and it came true. My cat was fine in the morning, and I've been a believer in answered prayer ever since.

I am well aware that we do not always get what we pray for, so it's easy to get discouraged when our prayers aren't answered in the way that we envisioned them. Solutions to problems don't always just materialize. Things don't happen miraculously as we'd sometimes like them to. There were many times in my life when I longed for things to go the way I'd imagined, only to be disappointed when they didn't, but there have also been times when the end result was even better than any idea I could have come up with!

The content of what I am praying for isn't always important. That I believe in a connection within myself to something larger than myself is what it's about for me. Believing in something larger and greater than myself allows me to let go of my pain and give it up to a higher power when life spins out of control.

Going to church on Sunday is meaningful to me, but that's not necessarily so for everyone. I go because I want to, not because I have to. For me, it's a place to go where I am surrounded by people of similar beliefs. I feel loved there. I belong to a sweet little Episcopal church with a congregation of friends who've supported me in times of need, laughed with me when I was happy and comforted me when I was sad. I am often touched by the music and the words of the sermon by my dear friend, Father Bill. I find it the best way to end one week and start another.

Whatever your belief system is, it's good to be able to call on your faith during the difficult times. I don't disagree with anyone's way of expressing their own faith, or lack of it, for that matter. My husband Walt hardly ever attended church services, even though he went to church every Sunday when he was growing up. He remarked on Sunday (his only day off), as he was getting into his canoe, that if God wasn't on the lake, he didn't know where He was!

My faith has gone through a journey where I doubted and searched, as I think most of us have at one time or another. To question is part of our nature as human beings. It's hard not to question "why" bad things happen. Sometimes people blame God. It helps to have someone to blame when a tragedy has occurred and we are searching for a reason.

Grief is something that can leave us feeling totally out of control in our little boat on the seas of life, faith is a bulwark against its storms. It reminds us that we are not in control of everything. I have an aphorism on the door of my refrigerator, displayed among the photos of my family and friends. It reads, "You are not totally and completely responsible for absolutely everything! That's my job. Love, God."

I see that saying every day, each time I open the refrigerator, and still I tend to think that I'm somewhat in charge. Then, along comes one of those days when I know I can't possibly handle everything that's churning around in my head, and that saying speaks to me. I laugh at myself, remembering that I'm really not in charge of everything at all and I give up trying to figure things out, at least for a while!

I MET YOU TODAY

I met with your soul today
while on its way through life
it intertwined with mine.

I brushed by your heart today
while on my way to share
a joy beyond belief.

I found you again, my Love,
so deeply etched in me
that boundaries had no place.

I sang from within myself
as I passed through your form,
emerging sorrow-free.

I won back my faith today,
so mirrored in your eyes,
my life became renewed.

I lay in your arms today
and heard you say my name,
a whisper in your sleep.

With you I set sail today
to places yet to be--
for now, still undefined.

I met you again today,
the same, yet all complete,
my faith in what will be.

Chapter 6

"If you had not suffered as you have,
there would be no depth to you as a human
being, no humility, no compassion."
Eckhart Tolle, <u>Stillness Speaks</u>

I always hated nursing. We used to take aptitude tests in school to find out what we were really interested in, and I never checked the little box that had anything to do with nursing. Yet I ended up being a nurse to two husbands when they were terminally ill. I can't say that I ever came to like it. At best it was something I dealt with because I had to. If you had asked me earlier in my life if I could have done the things I had to do to make my husbands comfortable, and see to their needs when they were so ill, I would have told you that I could never do it.

However, I started out gradually in my role as caretaker. My husband, David, was in remission for a few years after having been diagnosed with lung cancer and going through his treatments. At that time he was perfectly capable of taking care of himself, so the nursing part didn't start until a year before he died. Still, he was always in some kind of pain, and I wished I could do something about it. I can remember him saying, "What I wouldn't give for one day without pain." What I wouldn't have given to be able to hand him one perfect day, without pain.

One of the things that made me angry with him was the fact that he never stopped smoking even though he had been diagnosed with lung cancer! Although he was brilliant, he was also very stubborn. He was a systems analyst back in the days when the company computer filled a whole room and very few people owned personal computers. David had grown up in England, in Dorset, and had served ten years in the British army. He was born in Wales, and would always say that he was Welsh, a fact he confirmed with his resonant singing voice.

I had met him when I was a waitress, working at a Howard Johnson restaurant that was open all night. I had been divorced from my first husband for a few years, and had found the need to work at night to help support my four children. David came in regularly for breakfast after working late at night. There was a kind of mystery and excitement attached to the fact that he was tall, dark, and handsome, with a British accent to boot! Even though I had made myself a rule that I wouldn't date a customer, I finally gave in and went out with him after he persisted in asking.

He picked me up for that date at the Little League baseball field where I was working the snack bar during my son's game. He strolled up to the snack bar with that confident stride that I came to know so well, dressed in a pin-striped, three piece suit. To top it all off he was wearing a bowler hat and carrying a long, black, umbrella! I was incredulous and had to admit to those whose mouths dropped open along with mine, that this was my date for the evening!

Somewhere along the way, I think David became disenchanted with life. I think more than anything else he was homesick, not only for his native land, but for an England he'd known too many years ago for it to ever be the same. He took me there before we were married, and

I fell in love with the place and the people, but he was saddened by the fact that it wasn't the same as it had been when he'd lived there.

When he turned 40, he became reflective about what he had done so far in his life. He was such a genius that at 12 years of age (in the early 50's), he had built a television set completely on his own. He had always hoped that he might become famous for something he'd invented. Once he told me that he hoped to see his name up in lights (so to speak) someday.

I don't think he ever realized that he didn't need to be famous to make a difference. Once he taught computer classes to a group of paraplegics, for free, and they invited him to their graduation ceremony. He was astounded when they honored him for his contribution to their education. I doubt that he was aware of the difference he had made in so many lives by doing that.

David was an enigma, so it was very hard to discern what was going on inside his head most of the time. All the love in the world didn't seem to be able to penetrate. I think he was disappointed when life didn't go the way he wished it would. He was hardest on himself.

He decided to leave his job with the utility company where he'd been employed since we'd gotten married, and go out on his own as a consultant in his field. He left home to try to make his mark and "find himself," as the expression went in those days. He took a woman with him who had worked in the same office for many years. She was a great help to him, plus she admired his considerable genius and thought the world of him.

It was a very difficult time for me when he stopped living at home. He'd go out of state for weeks at a time, and although we kept in touch while he worked on consulting jobs, I only saw him now and then. I had a paper route along with my two older boys, because times were difficult financially, and there was very little cash flow. In spite of the fact that it was hard to get up early in the morning to deliver newspapers, especially in the winter, it was a godsend to be able to go and collect money from customers when we were out of bread and milk! Looking back, I shake my head in disbelief, when I remember the three of us starting out on a winter morning, while it was still dark and trudging through the snow. At that time it wasn't fun at all!

I've read that we may have dormant cancer cells in our bodies kept in check by our immune systems. I think that when our emotional well-being is at a low, our immune system is compromised, as it is when our physical health suffers. David's particular burden of sadness seemed to weigh heavily on him and no doubt acted as a catalyst for the disease, along with other physical factors. Together with his life-long smoking habit, the ground was fertile for lung cancer to materialize.

After the diagnosis, which he received during a doctor's visit to check a small lump on his neck, he returned home and worked at consulting jobs in the area so that he could have chemotherapy and radiation treatments. The woman who had been his co-worker was still there to help him whenever he needed her and was very much in the picture. Since she was in his company a good deal of the time, people who didn't know us well thought we had a very strange relationship.

David had a good friend who looked out for me and my children when he was away. He spent a lot of time with us, buying groceries, staying for meals, taking us places, and making sure we were well taken care of. He was a very special person. I don't know how my children and I would have survived without him during those rough times. Because he was around a lot, it was not unusual to see us all out together in public, an odd foursome, indeed. Strangely enough, he died a year after David did.

I knew in my heart that the woman who worked with David was in love with him, although he refused to believe it. I worked very hard at not being jealous over their being together so much. Because it was a constant battle inside of me, I sometimes had a hard time being pleasant when I was in her company. Once, when David was in the hospital for a new chemo treatment, she arrived just in time to hear the doctor talk about what was going to happen. We sat there listening, she and I, just as if we were both married to him.

The truth was that both of us loved him. I came to realize that she was as devastated by what was happening to him as I was. My heart began to feel a bond with hers. There was no longer any room for jealousy or anger toward her, not when life hung in the balance. We were two women who cared about a man who was very likely to lose his. I decided it was time to stop spending useless energy on anything negative.

After David's death I met this woman for a drink and conversation. We each brought with us half of a dollar bill that he had torn and given us once when we were all together. I think he meant for us to get together afterward and I've always been glad that we did. Everything that had gone on before was just water under the bridge, moving on and out of sight. I have kept in touch with her over the years since David's death and have always been glad that

I was able to let go of my earlier resentment of her. The benefits of doing so were a sound investment in my own peace of mind. Anger and resentment eats away at you. Forgiveness heals.

During the last four months of David's life I don't know whose pain was more intense, his or mine. I had to clean and dress the hideous tumor that had erupted out of the lymph glands on his neck. His pain was physical, but mine was located in every corner of my heart. How I longed to be able to alleviate his pain. Each day I experienced the depth of my own despair while I cleaned and dressed the deplorable tumor. It looked exactly like you'd expect a cancerous tumor to look, except they're usually on the inside, not staring at you on the neck of someone you care about.

I had a mantra that I would say to keep my mind occupied while I performed this task. It was from a little cross-stitched verse that sat on the mantle, near the recliner that David lived in during the last months of his life. It read, "Nothing shall come my way today that God and I cannot handle." After repeating it many times, I'd say the Lord's Prayer over and over again until I'd finished the job. This practice kept me from screaming out loud in anguish.

The day that David died, I knew it was time for him to leave me. People say that happens. I never knew what it meant until that day. I had gone a long time thinking and hoping that he'd be the one to overcome his cancer, or that some new treatment he was trying would miraculously make a difference, but in the last month of his life I knew I had to switch tracks. I had to do it, not only for myself, but for his family back in England, who hadn't seen him for two years. Most of all I had to do it for our seven-year-old son, who was always asking me if his dad was going to get better.

So near the end when Brian would ask me, I had to tell him that not everyone got better when they were as sick as his dad was. It broke my heart to also have to tell him that his dad might not be with us for very much longer.

The day of David's death, I had put on some music that I knew he loved. He sat in his favorite chair with his eyes closed and the blanket pulled up under his chin. I observed him and wondered how I would know when he died. I had kept him at home the whole time, promising him that I would never send him to the hospital as long as I could take care of him. Once, when I couldn't stop the bleeding in the tumor, I had had to call 911 to take him to the emergency room, but I made sure I brought him back home when everything was alright.

One fall day I knew that I had finally come to the place where I wouldn't be able to take care of him much longer, and on that day he died. When I felt for the pulse in his neck, I realized that I had never been with anyone when they died. I was just over forty years old and David was forty-five.

As I stood there looking at him, tears streaming down my face, something strange and wonderful happened. I heard his voice speaking to me. It isn't an experience I can describe well enough to do it justice. I can only say that it was as if his voice was speaking to me from the ceiling, only I heard it inside my head. He said as clearly as anyone could have ever said anything, "It's okay, I'm alright now. Thank you for taking care of me. I know you love me." Then he was gone, really gone--but I will never forget the joy and peace I felt from the experience of his passing.

OUR HEARTS' SEASONS

Red and gold wears autumn,
with leaves along my lake,
paddling through the breezy caps
nothing seems at stake.

Sure and fast my eyes stay
locked upon the road,
hoping you will surely come
release my heart its load.

Memory comes unbidden
of days so fast gone by,
spent perfecting this our love
without the need to try.

Steamy days of summer
with time caught on the run
fleeting in their memory,
setting with the sun.

Walks along the ocean,
so firm, your hand in mine,
floating in my vision.
So true, this love, so fine.

Lonely days of winter
with distant lure of spring.
Safely kept, my heart is yours,
its promise lingering.

Time and change, our seasons
like life along its way,
finds us in the scheme of things:
our hearts truths to obey.

Chapter 7

"I like living. I have sometimes been wildly, despairingly, acutely miserable, racked with sorrow, but through it all I still know quite certainly that just to be alive is a grand thing."
Agatha Christie

Nothing can prepare you for your first real experience with grief over the loss of a loved one to death. It is not rivaled by any other time of sadness. It takes precedence. Grief is, "keen mental suffering over affliction or loss, a cause of sharp or piercing distress or sorrow, abject despair." Anyone who's ever dealt with it can feel the impact of that definition.

It's totally bewildering to exist in such a sad state, and it's hard to know what to do about it. Like so many of life's events, there are no manuals to tell you how to live it or how to get through it. Some people are open to suggestions from others for dealing with their loss and grateful to have others around to help in their time of need. Other people may simply shut down and become oblivious to those who may be trying to help.

What I do know about grief is that it has to be worked through by going right into the middle of it, feeling its cloying sadness deep inside and facing it head on. There is no avoiding it by skirting around the edges or blindly passing over it. You can't just banish it. It has to be experienced in all of its various stages: sorrow, numbness, anger, loss, and pain. During the time we travel through its confines we experience a variety of emotions within ourselves that help us sort out what the loss means to us. It's imperative to be tolerant and patient with yourself during that time.

In spite of what kind of loss we are grieving over, most of us react the same way. We find ourselves in a place where we feel totally out of control, devastated and shattered by it. Whether it is the loss of a spouse, a child, or other family member, a friend, a relationship, a pet, a job, or even a dream, a feeling of helplessness invades our being. Within our devastated state we are all the same, no matter what the reason for the grief.

In the beginning, after a loved one has died, the hardest thing is just to get out of bed in the morning and start the day. Even though you may not feel like it, even though you may have no desire to do anything, you must. It is in the action of doing that which we are sure we can't, that we are able to overcome the apathy. With the physical act of putting one foot in front of the other and starting on your way, you eventually find yourself involved in doing something or meeting someone and alleviating the pain, for a little while at least.

Although I never kept track of all the people who spoke words of encouragement and had meaningful conversations with me during my times of need, I know there were many. I know that their words and caring meant a great deal to me. I didn't keep a count of the number of inspirational and uplifting books that came my way during those days either. Each one seemed to arrive when I needed it most, often given to me by a friend or appearing before me as if by magic. People prayed a lot for me too, and I know it helped because I often felt an unexplainable sense of peace come over me, a warm blanket of love, hope, and gentleness.

How long it takes to get to a place where you feel you have recovered after the loss of a loved one, whether by death or parting, is immaterial. The time frame is different for each individual. The important thing is to take time to grieve, take time to heal. Because we live in an age that doesn't promote spending a lot of time grieving, it might feel like allowing oneself to grieve may be too self-indulgent, but it isn't.

Sometimes it's difficult to find a way to make grief subside to a place where it no longer hurts when memories surface. Grief is a wound in the emotions that can be healed but will always remain a scar. The time it takes for the wound to heal is an entirely personal journey for each person who goes through it.

When I was immersed in mourning, every once in a while I would allow myself five minutes to go down to the depths of my sadness, to touch the rawest part. I called it 'wallowing', although I'm not sure if that was the appropriate word. Wallowing was so tempting to me because it loomed as the promise of something I deserved for my suffering bit it also threatened to be an indulgence that would send me into a dark abyss if I allowed too much time for it.

Understanding about pain and loss is not restricted to the sorrow a death brings about. Real loss and real pain are born in the human soul and reside within the emotions. That kind of wound is as real as any physical wound. The difference is that the emotional one is more dependent on love to heal it. Love is a balm for healing.

A teenager once asked me what I thought we were here for. I told him that I thought we were here to see what we could do with what life handed us, and that we were all faced with different challenges. What we did about them and how we lived our lives, determined who we were. It also played a significant part in how we viewed ourselves in the long run.

I think one of life's major challenges is the way we deal with grief. It's a real test of faith, endurance, and perseverance.

ॐ

SOMETIMES

Sometimes, in the darkness of the sunshine,
I have to go and find your words
to obliterate the heaviness of the air I plow through.

Sometimes, in the sharp sting of the stars
and the piercing of the moon,
I have to still my heart and help it find your love.

Sometimes, even in the sweet air of spring,
I have to go and find your smile
to blot out the pungent sadness of the breeze.

Sometimes, in the center of activity,
I have to close my eyes and feel your soul
to fill in the hollowness of the motions I exert.

Sometimes, when worldly logic makes no sense at all,
I have to go and sit on the steps by the lake
to remember things that defy logic.

Sometimes, when stoicism loosens its grip on my life,
I have to take up my journal
and write of thoughts denied and feelings unexpressed.

Sometimes, amid these moments in my days,
I simply have to search and find a truth
that helps me live through all my sometimes.

Chapter 8

"You have the greatest chance of being happy
when you respond to your own voice."
Sonya Friedman

When I was 18 years old, I wanted to write stories all the
time. I thought I had such a vast store of knowledge from
my life's experiences up until then, that I could almost write
a book. Now that I really do have a vast store of knowledge
from my life's experiences, I look back and wonder how I
could have ever thought that I had so much to call on at
age 18! Maybe the way I felt about my life back then was
simply an indicator of things to come.

I fell in love during college when I was 17, and after a
year I was positive that this was the man I would eventually
marry. It wasn't. When we broke up, after being together
for over a year, I had my first real experience with grief. I
can still remember feeling numb as I walked around the
campus without him. I can vividly recall the pain I felt
inside when he didn't even acknowledge me as we passed
each other on our way to and from classes.

Since then I have felt empathetic toward anyone who
has suffered a nervous breakdown. I know that I came very
close to having one at that time. It's a scary feeling when
you know that you are balancing on the edge of your sanity.
When trauma strikes it often leaves you feeling helpless in
its wake, and sometimes the mind just wants to let go and fly
free of all the pain. Holding on to my sanity at that moment
was the most difficult task I had ever encountered.

I can remember distinctly, standing in front of a rack of books in the library. Inside my head was a wicked desire to clear the shelf with a sweep of my arm, scattering all of the books on the floor. The thought was not logical. At that moment, I was keenly aware of the fine line that was separating me from a breakdown and for a split second in time I wanted to cross that line. All I wanted was to make the pain go away and tumble into oblivion.

Fortunately, I had a good friend with me at the time who could tell by the wild look in my eyes that I was about to lose it. He took me out of the building and walked with me, talking me through and out of my panic. I knew at that point that the little voice inside my head that had urged me to let go could be kept under control if I just remained calm. I knew I just needed to go about my days as if nothing out of the ordinary had happened to me. If I kept telling myself that, I could pretend it was so until the time came when I could handle the reality better.

So I survived, and when my parents announced that they could no longer afford to send me to college, it was almost a relief. A heavy sadness settled over me though, because I hated to leave all my friends. Still, leaving meant I wouldn't have to run into a certain someone on a daily basis. I wouldn't keep opening the wound in my heart. Going home meant leaving some of my sadness behind and starting over again.

I saw this man again, later in my life, when we were both married to other partners. I had gone to visit his mother and sister while on vacation, and his sister took me to see him at his office. Fortunately, I was happily married to my husband, Walt, at the time, because when I saw him and talked to him, my heart did little flip-flops. I think that old loves occupy a special little corner in our hearts where they reside throughout our lives. Seeing them again evokes thoughts that are tied in ribbons of remembrance.

I left college, went home and got a job in an office. I was determined to save some money so that I could go back to school. Instead of going back to school, I ended up marrying my boss, one of the two single men in the building where I worked. Six years my senior, I considered him to be very worldly in comparison with myself. Best of all, and probably one of the saving graces during the 10 years of our marriage, was the fact that he always made me laugh.

I married him for all wrong reasons, but I have never had any regrets about it. I ended up with three wonderful children as a result of that marriage. I look at how young I was at 20 when I had my first child and marvel that I knew anything at all about being a wife and mother! Youth assumes. I assumed that because it was what I'd always wanted, I would just know how to do it well and everything would work out fine. How innocently I entered into it all completely astounds me today!

My husband and I grew apart after a while. I wonder if we ever were close to begin with. We occupied opposite ends of the spectrum. My worldly husband was a salesman through and through, and he loved to be on the go. What I wanted most was to be a good wife and mother, happy to be at home. It was what I had always aspired to be. By the time I was 25 years old, I was the mother of three children.

I never really grieved the dissolving of my first marriage. I knew, somehow, it was the right thing to do, even if it meant that I was going to be raising my children alone. Back then that wasn't as acceptable a situation as it is today. I had been alone a lot when my husband was traveling with his job, so it seemed to me that it wouldn't be very different being totally on my own.

There was one poignant moment when my husband came back from his frequent travels and brought me two gifts: a book of poetry and a beautiful leather beach bag. I was incredulous, not because he brought me gifts but because of his choice of gifts. He had obviously given some thought to what I would like, yet it was so out of character for him. He had always made fun of my love of poetry and scoffed at my frequent trips to the beach. Thinking he might be trying to make some kind of amends, I asked him if he'd like to go to counseling with me. He replied flatly, "No".

In retrospect, I wonder why I didn't make more of an effort. The two of us are still friends today, although I only see him and his wife at family occasions. Sometimes I wonder why I wasn't more assertive about what I wanted and needed from him when we were married. Mostly, I blame it on my being young and immature.

I'd had a miscarriage, which had made me very sad, even though I already had three children. I had been hurt by his lack of sympathy over our mutual loss. Looking back on that Thanksgiving Day I spent in the hospital after miscarrying, I have a vivid picture of that 27-year-old woman I was. I see her sitting in the bed, not making a sound, tears streaming down her face, grieving silently for a child she'd never know. I would subsequently have two more children, but every once in a while there would be a reminder of that day when I lost my unborn child.

Later on, when I was first married to my husband David, I had another miscarriage. Although both incidents were sad to me, I didn't dwell on them--feeling that when that kind of thing happens, there must be a good reason why.

Nevertheless, that particular kind of loss always remains with you. It's the questioning of what might have been. It's about the loss of a child who would never get a turn to be born and be part of your life.

I AM YOURS

I am yours.
Thoughts of you propel me into my soul.
Visions of your beautiful smile sustain me.
Your loneliness without me, brings my own longing
full circle around me.

Penetration of your words and feelings,
have sliced through my very being.
I sit and let you wash over me like a balm,
with a soothing, healing affect
on my life's sorrows before you.

Everything seems to have been leading me to this place,
gently, but firmly forcing me always onward,
as if in some obscure part of me I knew
that you would be there at the end of my rainbow.

I love, to my heart's delight, you...
you, who are the culmination of all my longings.
you, who satisfy all that is within me.
you , who are a reflection of myself, as I see me in your
eyes.

Those eyes meet mine, holding them, probing their deepest
depths,
and at the same time our souls meet, pulling each other
closer.
Sparks of the heavens come down to earth,
igniting us in our entirety.

We create together a union so pure and timeless,
that it will abide within us forever.
Be always with me, as you are today,
and my soul will know joy through eternity.

Chapter 9

"We don't lose faith in the goodness of life because we become angry or depressed. We become angry or depressed because we lose faith in the goodness of life."
Susan L. Taylor

A woman called me one time after her husband had died to ask how I had managed to get through it all. She was a young woman who had married an older man, and together they had had a daughter. Her husband had died of a heart attack, and she wasn't dealing well with her grief. When she told me that she just didn't want to get up in the morning and face the day, I told her I understood. I suggested she try my practice of getting out of bed and starting the day even when she didn't feel like it. I told her that if she just kept going, in spite of not wanting to, she'd eventually find it easier to do.

She had a young daughter to take care of, and she told me that was the only thing that kept her going. It was good that that was the case. She had someone else to think of other than herself, someone who needed her. Children give us reasons to go on, even when we have no desire to do anything but curl up and die.

The way we present ourselves to them also determines how they deal with their own grief, which is often accompanied by bewilderment and guilt. When someone who's close to a child dies, the child often feels responsible, especially if they think they might have done something to displease them, or that it might not have happened if they'd been good. Being mindful of the sensitivity of the children when a spouse dies is very important. Often, we are so wrapped up in our own grief that we're not always aware of what they are going through.

Children need our protection, our understanding, and our love. It's the foundation of their security. If you have been hurt through a divorce or separation, it's especially important not to let a child feel any responsibility for what has happened. When there are hurt feelings or anger toward a former spouse it's essential not to project those feelings onto the children. Anger diminishes the spirit and takes its toll on wellbeing.

During the pain that accompanies divorce children are often trying to figure out where they stand and who they are. If their parents act hatefully toward each other it affects their self-confidence. Belittling an ex-spouse in a child's presence only ends up hurting them, not the ex-spouse.

Taking care of oneself is equally as important as taking care of the children in any situation that is associated with a mutual loss. For all our sakes, especially during the sad times, I would take my children to the seashore because I had spent so many happy times there when I was growing up. I would let them run and play on the sandbars all day long, while I sat in my beach chair reading a book or knitting. When the tide was low I never had to worry about them. Sometimes I'd run on the sandbars with them, just like I did when I was their age.

I'd pack up a lunch, but I'd also bring my little hibachi to cook something for supper, because we'd usually stay all day. When I worked as a waitress at night I was often tired during the day, so it was also a good place to go and be able to take a series of small naps. It was wonderful to sit in the sunshine, smell the marshes and the sea air, and be with my children--a respite from the problems of bringing them up on my own.

Because I had been happy going there as a child, I knew my children couldn't help but be happy there also. What an unbelievable treat it is for a child to be able to get wet, muddy, and covered with sand, and never be told once not to! When my sister and I took her small grandson to the sandbars for the first time, he looked around incredulously as if to ask, "Is all this for me?" Then with a broad grin, he began to run as fast as his little legs would carry him. My sister and I were as happy as he was, remembering just how good it had felt when our little legs were flying.

Getting through life's trials is about perseverance, but it is also about keeping your heart like that of a child, free and receptive to all the good things life has to offer. It's about taking in the joy and wonder of it all, not only through our own experiences, but through those of our children and grandchildren too.

ABSURD

It is contrary to all reason that I should have to
live my life without you.
It is contrary to common sense that you
should have to live without me.

It seems contrary to all reason that
I should have to wander on alone,
and contrary to common sense that you
should have to breath without me.

The absurdity of such a way of life
seems foolish at times,
while the foolishness of such a lifelong task
often seems absurd.

In truth it is not so--the absurdity of this
seemingly contrary existence.
It is instead a tribute to the heart's safekeeping
of a love that endures.

The simplicity of the heart is such
an easy thing to get in touch with.
The absurdity occurs only when
one doesn't recognize the heart's truth at all....

Chapter 10

"Our deepest fear is not that we are inadequate.
Our deepest fear is that we are worthy beyond measure.
It is our light, not our darkness that frightens us most."
Maryanne Williamson

A couple of years before I met David, I fell in love with a man who was a few years younger than me. He came into my life one beautiful summer day at the beach where I took my children. I think I knew early on that he would never be able to endure the commitments that went into years of marriage, but I loved him so much that for while it didn't matter. I was on my own with three children at the time and raising them well was very important to me. I knew that I could never choose to spend those years with someone who wouldn't fit into my plan. I wanted so much for it to be otherwise, but I knew in my heart it wasn't to be.

My youngest daughter was born out of wedlock. I suspect that people of her generation have never heard that phrase. Over forty years ago, when my oldest daughter was conceived out of wedlock, my first husband and I hurried to get married. We pretended for anyone who might be curious that we had gotten married in secret, for some obscure reason that I can't even remember today! At that time it was the thing to do. 'Out of wedlock' carried with it a stigmatism that was undesirable at that time.

Ten years later, however, I knew enough not to marry the sweet man who was my daughter's father. I was a forerunner, I think, of all those women today who don't feel they have to hurry up and get married just because they are pregnant. I knew from the start that I wanted the child I was carrying. I already loved her with all my heart long before she was born. I made the decision to have her, no matter what my marital status. Over thirty years ago that was quite a decision. Today, the adults of her generation would think nothing of my decision to have a child and not marry the father, whatever the reason. Many women today have a child first, even a second child sometimes, before deciding to marry. Some decide ahead of time to bring up their child on their own and have no intention of marrying. Today there are many choices.

Looking back on that time, I'm amazed that I was so strong. I made the decision to remain a 'single parent', a phrase not used yet back then. I made the decision in spite of all the odds against doing it. I've always felt it was the right decision, even though I was passionately in love with the man. Simply wanting him to become a different person than he was, couldn't make it so.

He was working at my favorite beach when I met him. I never knew until much later that he was A.W.O.L. from the naval base close by. What first attracted me to him was his gentle way with my three children, all under ten years of age at the time. My children were crazy about him and loved seeing him.

I think it was that same gentleness that caused him to become a victim when he served in the Vietnam War. The most sensitive men seem to come away from war the most scarred. There were so many men like him, who carried a certain sorrow and guilt around inside of them as a result of that particular war. Not only were they left with the residue of the war in their souls, but they came home to a nation that had mixed emotions about thanking them for serving in it.

It took me a long time to admit to myself that he wasn't husband material. I wasn't even sure he could bring himself to be good father-material, although I knew how much he loved his little daughter after she was born. I tried for a few years to make it be other than the way it truly was. I tried to believe he could change, come about and be happy, in spite of the sadness behind his eyes.

In that space of time when I knew him well, I spent time trying to fix him. I was very young and very idealistic. I was still positive that I had so many of the answers to a lot of the difficult questions in life. During the time I spent with him, there were coupled together more instances of joy and pain in juxtaposition than I had ever known before.

You can't fix another person, nor can you return their soul to them if they can't find it again for themselves. Of all the sorrows of my life, of all the 'what ifs', this is perhaps one of the most grievous to me. I could not make everything work out right just by wanting it so much, I couldn't make him well just by loving him with all my heart, and I couldn't change the way it was just by wishing I could.

I read something once that said, "God answers prayer in one of three ways: He says, "Yes," or "Not right now", or "I have a better plan." There would be a lot of better plans coming my way in the next thirty years and many more sorrows as well, but it was terribly hard to accept the truth of the situation at that time.

I've often regretted the fact that his daughter, had to miss out on having a relationship with her father after her early years with him. It was destined to be that way because it was his choice. Loving her could not keep him from subsequently becoming more of a loner than ever. At some point I stopped trying to orchestrate a relationship between them. In the long run, it was probably for the best, as he might have disappointed her often as he did me and my other children. He would promise to come whenever he was invited, but when he didn't show up, he was never able to give a reason why.

When I finally accepted the fact that trying to tie him down would be like trying to harness the wind, I let him go and moved on. By the time I married David, my little daughter was 4 years old. David loved her dearly and eventually became her legal guardian.

As parents, we can only do what we deem to be the right thing for our children at the time. We can't always be certain about the long term effects of any of our decisions concerning them. Still, when we make a decision about their lives, we have to be able to make it with the strength of our convictions. I remember my resolute self during that decision-making time, ready to go on with my life on my own, just determined to be the best mother I could for my children.

In spite of being deprived of the company of her father and her sadness in thinking he didn't love her, my daughter never lacked for love from me, her brothers and sister, or the rest of my family. Her father's family adored her, and even my mother-in-law from my first marriage loved her equally as much as her own grandchildren. Once she asked me if I minded her calling herself, "Gramma" to her. I told her I didn't think anyone could have too many grandparents! Love is the common denominator in all healthy children and adults. It's a very important factor in determining who grows up strong and intact.

ABOUT NEVER

Oh Love that lies so gently on my mind,
I cannot bear that I have lost the sight of you,
that I cannot even conjure up your image in my head,
but sadly so, have lost you to my seeing eyes.

And yet your very being never will be gone from me.
You are yourself in every fiber of my soul
and I have but to think of you
to feel your presence touch me as if there.

Then all the lonely waves lap gently on my shore
and comfort me that you were here for me.

Had I but known of what would be,
I would have hung on every word
and gathered every smile into my heart
to save for times to come.

I would have saved the warmth of you--
the step, the look, the laugh,
so ringing in me now.

If ever I can see your face and you again,
I will not waste such precious gifts.
I will not let them slip unnoticed by me.

No, I will savor every sound and look of you
to store away to comfort me,
from sadness on a far off day.

Then never will you go from me
without my knowing where.
Never will I let you keep yourself from me
and never will I let you go without telling you

How much I care.....

Chapter 11

"I want to know if you can be alone with
yourself and if you truly like the company
you keep in the empty moments."
Oriah Mountain Dreamer, The Invitation

I wonder if there's anything quite as beautiful and serene as snow falling softly on my hat and big bulky sweater as I walk outside in my clunky boots to put the mail in the box. I wonder, when the world is that quiet, sweet, and white, why anyone would want to think negatively. Excuses abound and people complain that they have to drive to work in it, go out to shovel, or plow it, but all the children are happy about being snowed in. I wish we could all be like children in that regard. The new fallen snow is so breathtakingly beautiful. I wish we could let go of any negative thinking about it, and just go out and walk in the white wonderland.

I want to feel the tiny flakes melt on my warm face as I turn it up to the thick sky. After I take a walk in it, I want to go inside where I can look out at the winter world, put some music on, build a fire in my fireplace and snuggle up on the couch. I want to do whatever I please because there's nowhere I have to go today. It's a good day to sit and be happy about where I am.

I suppose it's hard for some people to be happy about snow in March, when they are aching for spring to arrive. It's difficult to imagine warmer weather when the intensity of the snow and cold during the last weeks of winter dampen everyone's spirits. For me, snow always brings on wonderful memories of being young and skating on a big pond in the town where I grew up. It was a place where everyone would go and meet. We'd skate to the music playing over the loudspeaker and sit by the fire in the lodge afterward, talking to all our friends.

You can't live in New England all of your life and not have some fond memories of beautiful snowfalls. For the last a couple of years there were none. The winter has a kind of bleakness without the snow, but when it snows too much people aren't happy. They are definitely tired of it by the end of March. Everyone will come out of the woodwork when spring finally arrives.

The lack of sunshine on a snowy or rainy day causes a feeling of depression in some people. A sunlamp or a special light bulb that creates the feeling of sunshine sometimes helps. Other people, especially senior citizens, just can't take the cold weather and often go south or move to places where it doesn't snow. For those who suffer from depression, it's often a problem when they try to function without sunshine.

It's hard to imagine the kind of depression where even the beauty of Nature and the change of seasons can't lift your spirits. Remembering my despair in my times of dealing with grief, I suspect that depression must be something very similar to that. Grief is a window into depression, where you feel nothing can possibly make you feel better. You've been stripped down to your bare bones, feeling completely naked in its wake. Depression and grief go hand in hand when you can see no light at the end of the tunnel. When you can't even envision a place where you could ever be happy again it's extremely hard to get a grip on things. I empathize with those who suffer from depression and experience such feelings. It has to be very difficult when you can find no meaning left in your life.

At times, when life threatens to do me in, I go outside and look around. If it's in the winter, I go out and stand in my front yard and watch the falling snow and drink in the quiet. If it's a summer day, I might go out by the lake and survey the expanse of water in front of me, gazing across to the opposite shore where it meets the trees. On a cool spring evening I sometimes wrap my quilt around me and go sit on the steps by the lake, gazing up at that dark velvet rotunda overhead with millions of stars tucked into its folds.

I remember one time when I was feeling a little sad. It was late afternoon, and I had paddled out onto the lake in my canoe. I looked to the east where the clouds were edged in pink, from the setting sun behind my back. As I watched, they gradually disappeared into the deepening blue of the sky, and then I saw a faint golden light appear, as if caught in the branches of the trees bordering the lake

The full moon, in total defiance of the sun's performance in the western sky, was pushing its way through the tops of the trees. Determined and commanding, it slowly rose in all its majesty, lighting up the sky around it with a breathtaking brilliance. It played with my senses as I sat entranced by its slow and easy journey upward, where its size would soon become diminished in my view.

I sat there and thought about what a constant the full moon was. Although I existed in a perpetual state of change, I could always count on its abiding presence remaining unchanged at least once every month. It arrived in all its glory even when I wasn't there to welcome it, and it remained just as brilliant behind the clouds when it became obscured from my view.

When I sit outside at night and see the moon shining in the deep blue umbrella of stars overhead, I never tire of each extraordinary sighting and always welcome it with awe. I can count on it being bold and beautiful when it comes up over my horizon at night. It's done that forever. It will continue to do so long after I've stopped sitting by the lake and watching for it.

WINTER'S CHILL

Glossy pearls of windswept thoughts
blow across the frozen lake
where miles from the opposite shore,
they reach you,
brushing your heart with iridescent glistenings
of my love for you,
causing that waiting heart to quicken.

Could I but travel on the wind,
I would go there
and lay my head upon your heart
to hear its rapid beat.

Ensconced in the circle of your embrace,
I would lift my head to gaze at you
and kiss your mouth,
where no winter chill could ever rob the warmth
that sears my soul
and causes my spirit to soar.

No winter's wind nor landscape white
will ever find success
transporting frost into a place
where all the love the heart can hold
blazes on the hearth of who we are.

Chapter 12

"The time we share is never spent.
It lives in memory and brightens all
The days that follow."
Robert Sexton, <u>An American Romantic</u>

Once upon a time I had a brother. His name was Gregory Paul. He was born in September when I was a sophomore in high school. My sister and I were fourteen months apart. He was fourteen years younger than her. I thought his name was beautiful. My mom and dad and my sister and I had picked it out for him one Sunday morning as we all lay sprawled across my parents' double bed. Of course we also chose a girl's name because back then no one knew what sex the baby would be ahead of time. (I still like the anticipation of that mystery at birth.) It was a beautiful name for a beautiful boy. I'll never forget the thrill I felt that day in school when I was called out of class to the phone where my dad related the news of my brother's birth.

Greg was a happy and cheerful little boy, and my sister and I loved to take him with us in the car and to the beach. We loved to send him over to ask the lifeguard the time, a surefire way to get him to notice us without asking him ourselves! My mother doted on him, as mothers often do with sons. I think she was happy to have another child, because we were already teenagers when he was born and she was still quite young.

My sister and I both left home and married young so my brother grew up like an only child, as is often the case when there is such a span of years between siblings. Because most times it was just the two of them, my mother indulged him and let him get away with things she'd never have allowed when my sister and I were growing up. I once told my mother that he was a spoiled brat. This was after he kept poking me with a stick that I subsequently grabbed and threw away, much to his distress. When he began to cry, I was the one my mother got after!

We all loved him, though, including me. People always said that he had charisma. He was that kind of a little boy and that kind of a young man. My mother took him everywhere with her when he was growing up--to the parks, to the shore, and to any place her wandering spirit took her. She loved to roam the back roads of New England and find half-hidden picnic spots unknown to those who traveled the well-worn roads. My brother, in later years, referred to her as 'Anita Rand-McNally', because she could tell you how to get just about anyplace.

My father once told me that he felt badly that my brother had so much more than my sister and I had had while growing up. I disagreed emphatically, stating that my sister and I had had much more than he. Greg may have had more possessions, as happens in second families or children born later in life, but he definitely didn't have more fun growing up. Life was more of a struggle for my parents when my sister and I were young, but what I remember the most was the fun and the laughter. My brother ended up with more material things than we had had, but I don't think that made his life happier than ours had been in our young years.

Greg never got to experience a ride in dad's old pickup truck, traveling to my grandparent's lot at the lake. We used to go there on weekends in the summer. He never got to ride to the lake wedged between mom and dad like Fran and I did, one on the lap of the other. Although we squabbled about whose turn it was to ride on the top, it was always fun.

The memories of those times remain among my favorites. We sang songs and played games on our way to and from the lake. When we got there, we met up with our aunts, uncles, and cousins. Then we would all spend the day picnicking, swimming and having fun. We were never bored. I don't think we knew the meaning of the word. We never wanted more than we had, for it was always enough.

My brother drowned one summer's day, at 32 years of age, in a swimming pool where my mother lived. She, watching, thought he was clowning around as he often did, and waited for him to surface. Greg was an excellent swimmer, but my mom had never learned how to swim, so when he didn't come bursting out of the water for breath, she yelled for help. It was too late and too tragic, for the autopsy showed that he had died of asphyxiation due to extreme intoxication.

My brother was an alcoholic. My mother could never accept the findings from the autopsy, for if she had she might have also had to face the fact that she had often been an enabler to him. For almost a year before the drowning, he had gone through a period where he'd stopped drinking. It was a joy to be in his company during that time. All the sweetness that was part of his countenance was ours for the experiencing. Sadly, he succumbed to the disease. Although everyone found him to be a delightful, happy person, he actually had very little self-esteem. Because of that and his addiction, he left us much too early in his life.

In my experiences with grieving, I don't think I have ever reacted as angrily as I did to this unfortunate accident. Some people get angry with God, but I was angry with my brother. He had been careless with his life. He had taken away from us the joy that we had experienced in his company. Many times I had laughed so hard with him that I thought I'd split my sides! I remained angry with him for a long time for behaving as if his life meant so little to him.

He had been married and had fathered a lovely daughter. Even when divorced, he had spent many hours with her, taking her fishing and on hikes. She got married a few years ago at 24, and I was aware more than ever, that everything that was good about my brother was exemplified in his daughter. Now his daughter has a little girl of her own and sometimes it breaks my heart to look at her sweet little face and realize what my brother missed.

I guess because of my anger I could not relate to my mom's grief. I couldn't be around her when she cried and talked about him for she was like a lost soul. To lose a child has got to be the most crushing grief of all. My mom would have done and did do, almost anything for my brother. She would have gladly died in his place were it asked of her. I was angry with her even though it was not my place to judge her. I did, though, and in my judging found her, at fault in placing so much responsibility for her own happiness on him after my dad and she had gotten divorced.

I do not know--none of us can know--why it happens that someone so young dies needlessly. How do you come to understand such a tragedy? I think I got angry because I needed a place to expend my grief and, in being angry, I could handle it better. Anger is such a large aspect of grief that almost no death or mourning is exempt from it. Usually it subsides and leaves in its wake only sorrow over the loss and acceptance in the realization that no one is to blame after all. Life seems to take souls so often without any rhyme or reason. It's not for us to try to figure out the reasons why. Somehow, like everyone's life, Greg's life had meaning. For those of us he left behind, there are aspects of his life and interactions with ours that remain important and meaningful, stored away with our memories of him.

Because he was her child, my mom never really got over his death. We have photos of her at my niece's wedding a month before she died, smiling wistfully. In retrospect, I realized how heart-wrenching it must have been for her to watch my brother's daughter get married and wish that he were there to see it. I realized that I couldn't even begin to know or empathize with the grief a mother feels over the loss of a child at any age. In spite of my own times of grieving, I cannot even begin to imagine what that would be like.

Shortly after Greg's death, I was walking along the sandbars at the shore, and I saw a little boy running and laughing. A visual picture from my memory banks flashed, and I was back watching my little brother, many years before. He had run along those same sandbars, laughed, leaped, and loved the freedom one feels upon them. What a joy that picture of his little frame brought to my mind.

My brother loved to philosophize, and we had spent many an hour doing just that. I was reminded recently of something he once said about all of us being connected. He said that we are all linked together firmly, like the links in a chain, the chain forming a circle. The circle, strong and eternal, leaves no one dangling out alone without another hand to grasp. I realized at that moment how much our lives had always been connected and even though he was gone his life would always be linked together with mine. It was not my place to judge how he chose to live his life no matter how much I loved him. His life belonged to him. The choices he made were of his own free will.

SAND AND SEA

Old rusty time of days gone by,
Paid memory a call
And with it came a loneliness
I easily recall.

The orange haze of sunset ebbs
And leaves a lonely sea.
My eyes adjust their searching gaze,
But still there's only me.

The lacey waves pass simply on
Across my wandering feet.
To hear the sea all by myself,
Feels sadly incomplete.

The tiny waves now seem to pause
And puddle at my feet.
I feel suspended, lost in time,
As softly they retreat.

Now sand and salt and more than these
Will be my memory
Of one who loved the sea so much
And still walks there with me.

Chapter 13

"Man is born broken.
He lives by mending.
The grace of God is the glue."
Eugene O'Neil

Sometimes when my heart feels in turmoil, I have this uncontrollable urge to run away. It used to happen to me a lot when I was young and it still happens to me sometimes. When I was a little girl, I ran away one Christmas Day. I'd been quarreling with my sister and my mother had been scolding me. The whole business upset me so much that I felt a terrible urge to run away from it all to make it disappear. My mother handed me my coat and hat and let me go. Before I had even made it around the block I experienced some misgivings about it. I returned home, knocked on the door and told my mother I had come back for my new doll. She told me that the doll belonged to the little girl who lived there. At that point I burst into tears saying, "I want to be the little girl who lives here!"

I think that running away, or the desire to bolt free from a problem that is hurting my heart, is similar to the way I felt as a child. I was sensitive, and when my mother scolded me, my feelings were hurt. To feel like I could physically escape the hurt by running away made me feel like I could actually leave it behind in the dust of my flying feet.

Once, when I was in college, I had a falling out with my boyfriend, and the impulse to run away was so intense that

I just began to walk fast, leaving the campus and then the town, steadily moving toward a faraway destination I had in mind. It wasn't until I'd walked over half the distance to where my boyfriend's mother lived, that my feet, shod only in small ballet-like shoes, began to ache. At that point I began to doubt the validity of my plan.

The problem was that even though my original heartache had begun to dissipate with every mile I'd traveled, I had now gone too far to turn back. It wasn't until I'd walked 20 miles and the day was drawing to an end that someone stopped me and made a phone call to my boyfriend's mother. They were concerned because I was attempting to cross over the bridge from New Jersey to Staten Island on foot!

In the physical act of running (or walking fast) away from my pain, I feel like it can't hurt me any more. In the act of physically doing something, like walking, running, or vigorously working at a task, I can become detached from my problems and even solve them sometimes. As my mind is allowed to wander, engaged in the activity of the present moment, the pain begins to be replaced by determination.

I am still aware of that panicky feeling that comes over me in times of aching hurt. At such times I still feel that old familiar urge to run away. My thoughts urge me to do it, promising instant relief from pain if I can just leave the place I'm in. Nowadays I can jump in my car and go. I can simply drive away from sorrow or sadness when it threatens. There are many beautiful places of peace and serenity to drive to. Even though I live in a place that is full of peace and serenity itself, it is a familiar place and pain sometimes dictates that I escape the bonds of familiar surroundings to the unfamiliar.

One spring day I was raking leaves alone in my yard, feeling very lonely. Although the day was lovely with its promise of warm weather to come, buds to bloom into flowers, and birds chirping their song, I still felt lonesome. Sometimes the act of cleaning up the yard and working outside was such a communication with Nature, that it helped me when I was feeling blue. The time could pass swiftly, and the sun would begin to set before I even noticed the day's passing.

That day, it just didn't work for me, hard as I tried. As I rigorously raked, I felt like I just wanted to run away until my life changed and was more to my liking. I wanted to run away until I could be assured that when I returned, life would be all packaged up neatly and all would be well. I wanted to forget that I had to think, act, and manage my life. I was not doing well with any of those things, and that's what made me want to escape.

Disenchanted, I wanted to lose myself in the leaves. I wanted to go to a happy spot in my mind, roll up in a ball, climb into the lawn bag, and have someone cart me away to a fresh new place. I couldn't shake the running away feeling. I just wanted to be free of the task of figuring everything out. I wanted to be filled with wisdom about all the changes that were happening to me in my life. I wanted to know implicitly how I should deal with them and with myself.

It was all too much to think about. I had given it enough of my time lately. What did I really want? What was I searching for? Who in the world was I? It's funny to be so sure one day and so unsure on another. It's disconcerting to me that I am a creature of such immense contradictions that I am can be so easily influenced by my interactions with others, or that I can change so quickly from one mood to another as a result of a word, a touch, or a look.

It seems to me that I do a lot of this kind of stumbling along life's road. It stretches out before me, not as a long straight expanse of smooth pavement, but as a rutty, rocky, ever-curving, ever-changing pathway of hills and valleys. I am constantly disconcerted, wondering what's over the next hill. I have no way of knowing beforehand where the road leads, for no road map has been supplied.

A car full of people arrived in my driveway to interrupt my raking and my reflections. As they honked the horn and gaily waved at me, the change in my mood was instantaneous, proving how easily it could happen. Suddenly I had no desire to run away. The prospect of sitting a while, laughing and talking with friends, had completely obliterated my former state of mind. It was like a new day, and the possibilities were endless!

A WALK UP THE ROAD

I walk up the road.
The cold sweeps over me
in spite of my covers.
The day looks gray, as I trod on,
absorbing Nature as I go.
Puffs of snow on the cedars
wink at me as I stand, and watch
a cardinal gracing their branches.
I greet the horses, for they wonder
what I'm about today,
as they follow me with soulful eyes.
I cross the swollen, racing stream

and head on up the hill.
I run...
and once again I'm at the place.
Pebbles of memory turn to granite heights,
as I remember once again,
opening secrets with you, one steamy summer day.

I walk up the road.
The sun shines warmly on me,
for I have you beside me this time.
The day is bright as rainbows,
My hand is warm in yours.
The bare trees scratch the brilliant sky,
as dancing on I go.
The horses only glance our way.
They know what I'm about now.
The cardinal's graced another tree.
His beauty's in my sight.
I drop your hand and run once more,
off to find the place.
I stop...
I gaze at you from where I stand.
Sparks of memory bind us as we kiss,
while your arms for me a haven make,
and love's sweet promise walks with us, along our winter
way.

Chapter 14

"Reflect for a moment on all the past successes
and delights of your life: did you really know
in advance that life would be so good to you?"
Sonia Choquette, Ph.D., <u>Your Heart's Desire</u>

When I married my husband Walter, I thought how
blessed I was to know such happiness. He had been good to
my husband, David, and me when David was ill. For many
years, I had known him as a friend from the service station
and repair garage he ran with his uncle. When it became
extremely painful for David to ride in our old clunker of
a car, Walt had gone with me to buy a better car so David
could be more comfortable when I drove him to work.

Over the last year of David's life, Walt and I became
even better friends, talking about David's illness and Walt's
pending divorce. At David's request we even had Walter
over for supper one night. When he got up after supper,
he rolled up his shirtsleeves and began to wash the dishes.
I was very impressed with that gesture and thought how
great it would be to have a husband who did that!

When David died, Walt was there on the sidelines,
helpful and understanding. That's the way he was to
everyone. I was so grateful during that time, to have him to
call on. In true Walter fashion, he was always there when I
needed him. Years later, his sister told me that David had
asked Walt if he might consider looking after me when he
was gone. Walt had never told me that.

I remember one evening, a few months after David had died, when I had decided I was doing well enough to take up the task of going through some of his things. I had thrown a handful of his ties on the bed, and they lay there in a profusion of colors. What brought me back to another time, a time when David was alive and well, were the small pointed pieces of matching colors scattered among the ties. They were cut from the ends of the backs of all his ties and stapled onto pieces of cardboard that fit exactly into the breast pocket of his suits. I'd done that for him because he had always liked to carry a handkerchief in his breast pocket. His flare for something unique made him come up with the idea of cutting the ends off every tie so that he would have what appeared to be a matching handkerchief for each one.

At that point I lost it, and I began to cry. I cried many of the tears I had put away for another day. That day had come, and I experienced a loneliness that felt like it couldn't be assuaged. I called Walt. He came over right away, put his arms around me and said something that he would say often, all through the years he was with me. He said, "I think I have something you need", and proceeded to hug me.

Our friendship turned into something special and life took on a joy I'd forgotten existed. I had just come out of years of frustration with an illness that carried with it an element of despair. It had taken its toll on me. When grieving has been faced head on and discharged after finding it too heavy a burden to bear, there is no greater joy than to discover that life can still offer you its very best. For me, it did that with Walt. I married Walt a year after David's death. Some thought it was too soon, but I felt that when life offers you happiness after sorrow, you should welcome it with open arms.

Back when I knew that it was only a matter of time before the cancer claimed David's life, I wondered if I would ever find someone to be with after he was gone. I was only 40 years old. One day, while on a walk, I started to mentally list what I would be looking for in a man. I finally gave up in desperation and said, "God, you'll just have to take care of it for me. I can't possibly imagine how I will find the right person."

Soon after that, I had the answer to my prayer when I went to the garage to pay a bill to Walt. Framed in the doorway, tall and lean, with the light behind him, he smiled at me. Just as he did so, I suddenly heard a voice in my head say to me, "Here he is. This is the one." I was so embarrassed that I thought he would notice that I was looking at him strangely, but he didn't. When he and I started seeing each other after David's death, I related that remarkable happening to him, and told him I was pretty sure he was the answer to a particular prayer I had prayed.

COME WITH ME

Come with me you say
and I am happy.
Walk into the future with me.
Yes I will follow
you, who lift me up when I am sad,
you, who comfort me when I feel down.
Make me a portion of your life,
a part of you,
and you will make me whole.

Thank you, Love, I say,
for you fulfill me.
An essential piece of you I am,
saved from all your yearnings
through the years gone by,
safe for all the days to come,
Take me with you on your way,
and I will stay
close by you through it all.

Undying love you say, you'll give,
and I am thankful.
Still unfolding, life remains
that which I accept,
bringing us to where we meet as one.
I will find you time and time again,
with all the promise in your eyes
embracing my soul
and holding me through time.

Chapter 15

"When you know who you truly are,
there is an abiding sense of peace.
You could call it joy because that's
what joy is: vibrantly alive peace."
Eckart tolle, <u>Stillness Speaks</u>

I don't think I ever learned how to be as good a listener as I'd like to be, but I admire anyone who is. A friend, who lived next door to me when my children were growing up, was the best listener I ever knew. I wish that I had learned how to do that just from observing the way she did it. She did it so well. You knew when she was listening to you that her attention was focused completely on you. She had a way of making you feel like you were the most important person in the whole world.

Her husband was away from home for months at a time--something his job demanded--and so she spent a good deal of her married life raising her three girls on her own. I was alone a lot too because my first husband often worked at night, in addition to his day job. During the last couple of years of our marriage, he had to travel out of state because of a new sales job, and consequently, was only home a few weekends out of the month.

So, it came to be that she and I spent a lot of time together, comparing notes about our kids and our lives. We would spend hours talking over coffee while watching the kids play. That's when I came to realize that she was a better listener than I was. I was always anxious to voice my opinion or tell my own story. Often times my powers of concentration were lost in my haste to speak. My inability to concentrate on listening must have come from early on, when my desire to please and to be accepted was tops on my list of wants. The desire to be heard and to feel important brought on the compulsion to speak.

I loved my conversations with my friend, because I always felt special. I felt like what I had to say was important. I realize now that it was because she not only listened to me, but was truly interested in what I had to say. All the kids in the neighborhood loved her. She could get the boys to help her with any chore she needed assistance with. They were only too glad to do it, because she had a way of making them feel important.

Sometimes, with children and teenagers, in treating them as such, we don't give them the same time or understanding we would give to a fellow adult. She would always ask them about themselves, or about something she knew they were interested in, drawing them out of any shyness they might have had. Then she would listen attentively to what they had to say. She gave them the same attention and respect she would have given a grown-up. With that attentiveness, she helped them to increase their own self-confidence. I admired her for that.

It's especially important to be a good listener for someone who is grieving and wants to talk. Although people who are mourning are not always saying so on the outside, there are usually indications of what's going on beneath the words, discernable if you're paying attention. Most people aren't really looking for a response. It's the talking out loud about the grief that's essential to them.

After experiencing a loss, there is a tremendous need to talk about it or about the loved one. When my mother talked incessantly about my brother after he died, it was about a constant need to keep his memory alive, by always including him in her conversations. It was as if by doing so, she could keep some part of him with her.

Because of the need to talk when you are grieving, support groups are a great help. They are also important places for listening. It helps to listen to others who have had some of the same experiences with mourning. Everyone gets to talk about how they're feeling and listen to how others are feeling. Talking and listening to others who have also suffered a loss reminds us that we aren't the only ones it has happened to.

LOVE'S PULL

So if you pull away again,
I bend to let you go
And if your heart goes far from me,
I wait 'til you can see,
the part of you that's gone from sight
you've left right here with me.

But if I pull away from you,
you know what I must do.
And though it seems I've slipped your grasp,
you know it isn't true.
for all the times I let you go
my heart is still with you.

And so we venture off again,
a trial of things to be.
And though we try to work it out,
it still remains, you see,
that when we stand alone, apart,
joy isn't meant to be.

So joyously we meet again.
Our hearts are open wide.
And then we take each other in,
our souls are winging free,
for all the love our lives can hold
exists when you're with me.

Chapter 16

"Delight is high-level quality happiness.
It is a solid feeling of being permanently
connected to our own good."
Mark Victor Hansen & Barbara Nichols, <u>Out of the
Blue</u>

Walter. Where do I begin to tell about who he was? The memories of this special man are filled with his wonderful spirit, his quiet unassuming nature, his wry sense of humor, his unpretentiousness, and his loving heart. It's difficult even now, ten years after his death, to be reminded of what a treasure we all lost when he died. My son, Brian, titled Walt's obituary, "The Man Who Touched Us All," and indeed he did.

I think that I have put off writing about him, not because it is so painful to do, but because it is so intensely bittersweet in my remembering. I think I've even played down how happy a time it was, and how full my life was with him. I've played it down because that part my life is gone forever. My life may hold other treasures, other loves, and other experiences, but the experience of knowing and being married to Walt was all-encompassing, totally satisfying, and much too short.

Walter was unique. He was the man who matched the mental list I had made about the qualities I was looking for in a man. His most endearing quality was that he listened and paid attention. He paid attention to what I liked, what I said, and what I wished for. Then he would surprise me, not only by his astounding memory, but also by his thoughtfulness.

The first time I ever sat by the lake I love so much was after a hurricane had toppled so many of the trees there. Walt was living in his cottage on the lake at the time, as he was in the process of getting divorced. He had gone down to cut up the fallen trees and clear the debris in the yard at the cottage.

I had had a particularly difficult time during the previous few days because of the power outage at my house. Trying to keep David comfortable and warm without the use of his electric blanket, had been the hardest part. Trying to dress and clean the tumor on his neck had also been difficult without hot running water. Fortunately the weather had been warm and we did everything outside on the grill, including boiling water.

When the storm was over and the electricity restored, I went off to get David's pain pills that he had run out of. I stopped at the gas station and as usual, had a lengthy conversation with Walt. He talked about going to the lake and cutting up some of the many trees that had fallen down during the hurricane. In exasperation, I asked if I could possibly go down there and sit by the water for a while. I was very much in need of doing something calming. I'd survived the storm; it was the aftermath that was wrapping itself around me. Happily he said, "Sure", and wrote the directions to his cottage on a piece of paper for me. I still have them today, and the sight of his quick left-handed penmanship, sprawled across the page, tugs at my heart when I see it.

I needed to go somewhere quiet to regain some much needed peace, and forget about illness and nursing for a while. I left David with my oldest son, Mark, and his pregnant wife, Uschi, who were living with us. Mark was in the Army at the time and had recently been stationed in the United States after many years of being in Germany. He'd met his wife there and returned to the states with her just in time to have the Army and the Red Cross help get him attached to a base near home because of David's terminal illness.

I think it was on that day, about a month before David died, that I gave in and accepted the inevitability of his death. I had held off for so long, but on that day, on the way to pick up his prescription, I finally broke down and cried. That day when I sat on the steps, down by the lake, I cried again as I drank in its peaceful healing properties for the first time.

I looked down toward the end of the lake and saw a little white building by the public beach area. Somewhere in an 'all knowing' place, I saw myself looking down at that little building for years to come. There was no figuring out or reasoning to the feeling—just a quick and secure knowledge of a destiny yet to arrive. Now, when I look down the lake and see that little building, I remember a beautiful, clear, autumn day when I sat on those steps and felt like I'd come home. I also remember experiencing a feeling of unbelievable peace, even though life was crashing down around me.

There is a meaningful incident, so typical of Walt, from that day that also sticks in my mind. He had brought a bottle of soda down to the steps where I was sitting by the water. It was exactly the brand and flavor I always ordered at the gas station. He'd remembered and brought it with him to the lake for me. I saved the bottle in my cupboard for years as a reminder of his thoughtfulness, which had made such an impression on me.

He didn't say much to me while I was there. He simply allowed me to sit by the water and drink in its peacefulness, while he went about the business of cutting up fallen trees and limbs. The day was absolutely beautiful. After a hurricane the sky is usually cloudless and very blue. That day was no exception. I just sat there and let the warmth of the sun envelope me.

It wasn't only me who benefited from the powers of observation Walter possessed; it extended to everyone he knew. People who came into the gas station could count on him remembering their brand of cigarettes, how they took their coffee, and what was going on in their lives. His 80-year-old uncle who ran the station with him, used to get so aggravated with Walt because he spent so much time talking with the customers while pumping their gas. Walt knew all the news of the town and remembered all the history of times past. Sometimes, when I find myself wondering about someone or something that happened in town, just for a minute I think, "I'll have to ask Walt. He'll know", and then I remember that he is gone.

In the last years of his life, Walt, who was tall and slim to begin with, began losing weight and looking gaunt. I think it must have been very frustrating for him to accept that the physical man he had once been was no longer present. For me there was an innate sorrow beyond words. When a wife has to tend to the wasted body of a man whose muscles were once lean and hard, and whose body was known implicitly to her in its healthy state, there ensues a sense of unbearable loss. Watching someone you love waste away from a terminal illness isn't like growing old together where bodies simply age naturally. It is instead, an eye-opening observation of how disease can mock vibrancy, replacing it with weakness and dependency.

FOR FOREVER

Tied together for forever,
midnight blue and sunset red.
Whisper softly, shout out-loud,
teach the wind to blow away
clouds of sadness, clouds of gray.

Tied in circles through the years,
strung together, traveling through
inner highways, paths of truths.
Gathering mist you softly kiss
eyes that see each others' soul.

Safely guarded from all harm,
stores of treasure, housed by time.
Autumn's gold and winters' white,
springtime green and summers' blue
through the ages, keeping watch....

For forever.
two together, always one.

Chapter 17

"I have decided to stick with love.
Hate is too great a burden to bear."
Martin Luther King Jr.

A soft rain is falling on this summer day, and I don't mind at all. I sit on my deck under the big umbrella, gazing out over my lake and absorbing the beauty of it all over again. It feels different today; it's gray and cloudy. Children can't go out to play. I can remember being a child, staying with a friend at her grandmother's cottage. We sat there watching the rain pelt down, knowing we couldn't go out and swim that day, and I can remember wondering, "Why not?" What was the difference when we would get wet either way!

This morning I'm thinking about sitting down by the water or going swimming, with the sweet taste of rain falling on my face, teasing my senses as I float along. I sit at the table on my deck under the shelter of the big umbrella. The rain beckons me to come out and laugh while it showers me with its wetness. I've done it before. A hauntingly poignant memory escapes the confines of my treasure chest to remind me I've done it before: a broken umbrella overhead, a puddle of water under my feet, and the face of my Beloved laughing back at me as we got soaking wet and didn't care.

The rain is getting heavier. As the wind picks up, it tickles my back, the part of me outside of the umbrella's range. It's alright. I am serene like the lake with its polka dots of raindrops sprinkled evenly along its surface. I am sprinkled with random thoughts and know it is a good day for me. It promises to be a day without any sorrow. It's been very warm and the earth has been dry. Now the rain is watering the thirsty flowers and plants all at once. I've wandered around and picked off the old blooms before the rain ascended. Now, with their faces turned upward to the heavens, they look quite happy. Peace abides all around me in the stillness as the silent rain falls.

My day holds the promise of anything I wish to fill it with. What will I decide to do? I don't know yet, there are so many choices. I do know that none of them will include obligations, because I've promised myself a day devoid of all obligations. That means that I will not suffer any anxiety, unrest, tension, or worry, because I will be living the day only as it unfolds.

I have discovered that if I get outside of my mind and leave all fearful things out of my present realm, I can concentrate on the beauty of the moment and of the world around me. If I use my mind when necessary but allow my soul to come through more often, I have the ability right within my grasp to have all the happiness I seek. It's right here for the taking, bound up in this day, and since this day will never come again, why let it slip away so easily from my grasp, becoming part of the past?

Now, as I sit inside out of the rain, and look out my porch window, there is no forlornness as I watch the falling drops. I've written in my journal, recording how peaceful I'm feeling. I look over the books that I have been reading and wonder if I should be really self-indulgent, lie on the wicker sofa and read to my heart's content. Beside the sofa sits a basket spilling over with yarn, the knitting needles protruding out of the basket with their few rows of color, waiting to become a finished afghan. They beckon me also. I'm not quite sure which undertaking I want to embark on. All prospects seem enticing to me.

What I do know for sure is that life always beckons me onward. I live in anticipation of what may come to me around the next bend in the road. Having no idea lends a sense of excitement at the prospect of a surprise. Sometimes I conjure up scenarios in my mind, but then expectation arises. Having no expectation leads to less disappointment. How can I possibly know where the road ahead will lead when I don't hold all the cards.

So, I do the things that make me feel good. I do the things that feed my soul. I do work that I love and find it gratifying. I spend time with an old friend or make a new one, and I am reminded of how satisfying that feels. Each time I am in the midst of my family, especially when everyone is gathered together, I'm happy. When I finish something I've created with my mind or my hands, I feel a wonderful sense of accomplishment and satisfaction. Every time I love and am loved back, I feel blessed and that gladdens my heart.

RAIN

So deep in the quiet the mist softly falls.
I feel separate parts of me melding as one.
On the steps by the water hang echoes of thunder.
My parts, once converging, are hurling away.

To the east, on the storm clouds, my thoughts break apart.
My heart flies beyond to a place not so far.

I feel from that place something brushing my heart,
and with spangled emotions I'm turned inside out.

With my hair blown and soaking, I bend to the ground,
and wonder if life lives there hidden from view.
Can I still tread its landscapes and live without you,
while lovingly holding you deeply within?

Shall I look in the waters and find me your form,
while I rest from my labors and sleep in your soul?
Am I cleansed from my memories by mist on my face,
and steadfast as ever, though broken apart?

Rain on me, heavens, and bring me a balm.
Teach me to know again just who I am.
Swirl me in waters and spin me around.
Leave me to surface and taste the sweet rain.

I am washed of my grieving by rain on my heart.
I am solid as ever, though splintered and bare.
It is said that we make it, much stronger by far,
yet each time I do it, I still have a scar.

Quiet me, quench my lost heart from its depths.
Teach me again to emerge from its grasp.
Tell me the sunshine will find me again.
It is only through pain we are broken anew.

It is only through Grace that I live without you.

Chapter 18

"The quality of a life...the richness of its minutes...
is all that really matters. Only those moments touched
by care, effort, joy and love are of lasting value."
Robert Sexton, An American Romantic

My husband Walter died of AIDS. We didn't put that in
his obituary though, because hardly anyone knew about it.
We didn't say he died after a long illness either. We didn't
even say that he died of cancer, although in the middle of
being HIV positive he developed Hodgkin's Disease. At
the time, he was relieved to be able to tell people that he
had cancer, because it was an acceptable disease. So most
people believed he died of cancer. People saw him waste
away during the last two years of his life and assumed that
that was the reason for it.

What they didn't know was how valiantly this good
man battled this insidious virus that had taken hold of him
shortly before I started to date him. As with the first news
of my husband David's cancer, I can still remember vividly
the day I knew that Walt could very well have the HIV
virus.

We had only been married a couple of months when I
went to give blood (something I had done for years) during
a local blood drive. The questions for qualification had
changed, now including inquiries about sexual activity in
donors. The question that applied to my situation asked if
you had had sex with a man who had had sex with another

man. I can remember calling Walt and reading him the
question, then asking him if I should give blood. He said,
"No."

I walked out of there in a daze, seeing a panorama of
the years to come spread out before me. I had no real idea
what the disease AIDS was truly about at that time, except
that it was fatal. Back then, in l986, I knew very little
about the disease except what I'd learned from a speaker
at a church group. Even after listening, I'd found it hard to
comprehend how the HIV virus was connected with the
disease of AIDS. Later I learned that HIV is the virus, and
AIDS is the disease that takes over when the virus is full
blown, and the immune system is finally compromised.

It's funny the things that stick in your mind when you
recall the impact of monumental happenings in your life. I
had just had a birthday, and Walt's mom had given me some
money for a gift. I went to buy myself some shoes with
the money. I walked around the store, picking up shoes
and looking at them, subsequently putting them back
down, without trying any on. All of a sudden I came out
of my daze, and my eyes lighted on a pair of moccasin-type
shoes, cream colored with mauve and blue, exactly what I
was looking for. I tried them on, and they fit perfectly. I
bought them and drove home, still existing in my state of
numbness. I loved those shoes and wore them for years, but
every time I put them on, I was reminded of that fateful
December day.

I resigned myself quickly to the fact that if Walt was
infected, then the dye was already cast between the two
of us. I reasoned that since I loved him so, and knew we'd
always be together, we would never have to worry about
the possibility of infecting anyone else. The task of dealing
with it would be ours alone. Of course, I didn't know for

sure at that time that he was infected, but we found out four years later when a health problem brought about the test that indicated Walt was HIV positive.

Early in our relationship, he'd told me about a gay friend he'd been keeping company with before me. I think I knew, deep inside, on that day, that there might be a chance we wouldn't get to grow old together. We dated and became very close very fast. We'd already known each other for years, and talked about everything in the world when David was terminally ill, so we'd established a bond early on.

Walt had a very dry sense of humor. The doctor who would become our close friend through all of the years of his disease, asked the question that most people ask when they find out a person has AIDS. He said, "How did you contract the disease?" To this day, I'm always prepared for that question when people discover what Walt died of, and to this day it still gets to me. When someone learns you have cancer, they don't ask how you got it, but because AIDS is considered a behavioral disease, it's the first thing people want to know. I loved Walt's reply and I use it still. He said, "Well, my first wife was such a bitch that I thought I'd try something different!" And so he did. The result of doing so eventually brought about his death.

Many years after Walt's death, someone at a funeral asked me what Walt had died of, and I replied, "AIDS". She followed with the expected question. For a long time I used to tell people he had died of cancer. My own mother didn't even know, because it didn't seem necessary to tell her. We told Walt's mom near the end, because his father had just passed away, and we felt it was only fair to be honest with her. It was difficult for Walt to tell her, but he knew he had to.

She took it like a trooper, although it was very hard

for a woman in her 80's to comprehend the extent of the whole business of the disease. She loved Walt dearly, and once she knew he was terminally ill, she took an active part in making his last few months enjoyable. She still lived in the town where she was born, the town where Walt grew up, and knew everyone. Out of respect for her, I rarely told anyone except those closest to us, that he had died of AIDS. Sometimes I'd decide on the spur of the moment to tell someone, because of how our conversation was going, or just because I wanted to.

It's difficult to go through a grieving process with a lie at the forefront, but society and circumstance demanded it of us at the time. Today I find it refreshingly honest to tell the truth when someone asks. I also feel a bit duty bound about it, because it never felt right to lie or withhold the truth about it to begin with. I only did it out of respect for Walt's mom, because it mattered to her. Walt's Mom died a few years ago, and there was no longer any reason not to tell the truth. It seems especially important to me these days, since I find the need to address the lack of education and acceptance of the disease. To do that, I need to be upfront about my experience with it.

There were times when Walt was so ill and incapacitated during his last six months that I wanted to scream and yell at people, and tell them how awful it was that he had AIDS and couldn't even talk about it. However, if the truth were known, I'm afraid that many people would have had a hard time with it, might even have shunned him. He was never looking for sympathy anyway, but I thought it was a crime that he had to keep it a secret.

I can remember the little knowing look he'd give me when we were both working at the gas station, and one of the guys having morning coffee would tell a joke about

AIDS. He'd laugh along with all the rest of the guys, and my heart would go out to him. I often wondered what they would have thought if they'd known. I'll never know how many of them would have been supportive if they had. Many people are afraid of AIDS for various reasons, but mostly because they don't know enough about it.

It has to do with fear, and fear comes from ignorance and lack of education. Even though it makes me angry, I can understand it. AIDS is an insidious disease that demands a healthy respect of its consequences. It is a disease that many think will never touch them. People feel that it's something that will happen to someone else, to another person's family, but never to them. There was a time when we didn't think cancer would affect our lives, either. It happened to other people but not to us. Now there isn't a person whose life hasn't been touched by its consequences, whether in our own personal experiences or that of someone we know.

So it will be with AIDS. People think it's about someone else, not about them. They feel there is no need to be educated about a disease that will probably never affect them. They may be wrong, since AIDS is becoming a disease of epidemic proportions, affecting over 40 millions people today, worldwide. Tomorrow it will affect us all. AIDS is becoming more and more of a heterosexual disease, with the possibility of infection anywhere, plus the HIV virus is constantly mutating.

Walt fell in the cracks back in the days when he was first diagnosed. Attention was starting to be paid to groups who were at risk: gay men, IV drug users, and people who had received contaminated blood from the blood banks, before testing became mandatory. Walt didn't fit in any of those categories. He was not the usual candidate for AIDS.

When I began to research and find information about HIV and AIDS, it was 1990. There wasn't a lot of information to be found in mainstream medical books and periodicals. I had to dig deeper to help us out with our understanding and treatment of the virus and the disease.

I spent eight years researching this dreadful disease, its complications, and the treatments that were starting to be available. What I found was that the side affects of those treatments were, in many cases, responsible for lowering the immune system even more than this compromising disease was doing. I came to the conclusion that the best course of action was to try and keep Walt as healthy as I could, for as long as I could, before the virus took its toll and turned into full blown AIDS.

I'd like to think that I might have been responsible for keeping him around a little longer than he might have lasted, had he been taking drugs. During the years he was HIV positive, there weren't a lot of drug treatments available, and those that were hadn't been in use for very long. Near the end, when the "cocktail" drugs (combinations of three drugs) were just coming on the market, his family really wanted him to try them, and so he did. I'm not against them or their ability to prolong life, and today they are responsible for doing just that in many cases. However, in l996, there was still a lot to be learned about them.

I had chosen an alternative route to drugs for Walt. At the same time, we kept regular visits with our wonderful doctor at our HMO. Our doctor told me he didn't want to see me waste my money because alternative treatments weren't covered by our insurance. I told him that I had to explore every avenue available to Walt, and be actively doing something, or I'd go crazy.

I didn't go crazy, even though there were times when I

knew if I let go, I could have easily lost my mind. Mostly, I opted for keeping Walt well-fed with nutritious food, supplements, and natural medications. It worked pretty well until a year before he died, when he contracted an opportunistic infection in his brain, called, 'cryptococcal meningitis'. I knew he'd have to take a drug to combat that.

People with AIDS can contract all kinds of diseases that one has never heard of, because their immune system has been compromised. The immune system, when intact, keeps many forms of bacteria in our body under control. A compromised immune system allows for any number of previously unheard of infections to invade the body. They are called opportunistic infections.

From that time on until he died a little over a year later, Walt valiantly carried on as if nothing were wrong. That's the kind of man he was. There was a short period before he died where he rallied with the new drug treatment, and then his whole system simply crashed. Near the end, I had to help him with so many of his normal activities and daily hygiene that I despaired of ever being able to get through it all. Walt was so good about everything, always keeping his sense of humor, that I think I got some of my strength from him.

Once, before Walt got really sick, he had said to me, "If I ever get really bad, just shoot me". We don't have a choice about such things. We don't really have a choice about how we die, except maybe in preparing for it ahead of time if we know it is imminent. Walt only minded that he didn't know exactly when it would be--weeks, months or years. I don't know why he wanted to know that. He just went on living his life the way he normally did. I think he just wanted to have some idea about when it would happen.

When Walt's uncle who had run the gas station with him, died at 86--a year and a half before Walter did--it seemed like the answer to a prayer. With that occurrence along with financial reasons, we were able to close the gas station, (an institution and gathering place in town) and allow Walt to take it easy, while satisfying the customers with our sound reasons for doing so.

We took a couple of vacations, including one to Hawaii and one to Germany, where my son and his family were again stationed. People asked why we were taking so many vacations, and Walt's answer was so typical of him. He said we were taking all the vacations that he'd never gotten to take, during the years he was working at the gas station. After his death, when people asked me that same question, as I took off on yet another vacation, I answered in a similar way, only I said that I was taking all the vacations Walt would never get to take. Sometimes when I contemplate whether I should go or not, I can hear Walt saying to me, "Go for it!" That was always one of his favorite expressions when someone couldn't make a decision about treating themselves to something nice.

My heart broke when Walt died. I grieved for him for a very long time. I had known that he would die, and I had prepared myself for it, because I had lived daily with the knowledge of what was coming. I don't think I had any idea, though, how heavily the loss would weigh on me. With all my bustling about and matter of fact forging ahead with things, I'd told myself I was prepared. He had been sick for a long time, and my caretaker role had left me no room to imagine how sad the eventual loss would be.

After he was gone, I was alright if I didn't think about the fact that I would never see his tall lanky frame walk through the back door again. If I stopped expecting to see him come up over the hill and wave at me down by the water, I was okay. When such thoughts dared to surface, I had to push them back for fear of falling apart completely.

Coupled with my sorrow, though, was my anger at the ignorance of people with regard to the disease. It was an ignorance that might have kept some people away from Walt if they'd known he had AIDS. I never contracted the disease, although I had been very intimate with my husband from the start. Somehow, I knew from the beginning, that I never would. Maybe it was, in part, because I never worried about it. I had a healthy respect for the disease, got tested periodically and was careful when I should have been, especially near the end. I didn't harbor any fears about it, I just felt a tremendous sadness over the progression of the disease--not only in my husband but in the whole world.

Shortly after Walt died, I was walking along the water's edge in Myrtle Beach, because walking the beach was my solace. As I walked, I found myself thinking about how well I was handling everything. Mark, Uschi and my grandson, Patrick, had come with me for a time-share week that Walt and I had planned to use if he had been well enough. When the week was over, we were all going on to Atlanta to spend Thanksgiving with my daughter, Michelle, and her husband, Russ. There were things to do and thankfully, family to help fill in the gaping holes left in my heart.

Then, I saw a starfish on the beach, washed up by the tide, and the wall I had so carefully built around my grief crumbled. As I took in deep gulps of air, my heart began to beat wildly in my chest. I screamed silently inside myself, as I felt my heart scraped raw. It was a monumental task to find something else to think about to bring myself back to the present, back to my former feeling of security, and not think about the starfish at my feet.

At Walt's memorial service, Father Bill had related a story of a man walking on the beach, picking up starfish and throwing them back into the water. A friend who was walking with him asked why he bothered to do that, saying that it wouldn't make any difference since there were so many starfish washed up on shore. The man answered as he threw back yet another starfish, "It made a difference to that one."

Father Bill had said that was the way Walt was. He ever so quietly made a difference with each person he took the time to listen to or help. After his death so many people had related stories of special things he had done for them, stories sometimes that no one else had even known about. That was just who he was. I think he'd be surprised to know that just by being himself, he'd made a difference in the lives of so many of the people he came in contact with.

How could I not mourn the loss of that kind of man? How could I not grieve when his cheerful presence would never brighten my day again? That's what grief is like--the undeniable truth that we are in the midst of an almost unbearable loss. We are in the midst of a loss so crushing that we question if we'll ever be the same again. We are never the same again, because the connection of the life of someone we love with our own enhances ours. When we can no longer claim the joy of their company, because they have gone from us, we feel like we have literally lost a part of ourselves.

There is a long expanse of bridge over a wide part of the Connecticut River near where I live. Whenever I travel over it, a memory comes to me, bright as sunlight. It is a beautiful image of my beloved husband, a few years after I'd married him, tall and strong and vital. He was waterskiing behind a friend's boat on that river, one glorious summer day, and the sound of his laughter as he bounced back and forth over the wake still resounds in my ears.

SUSTENANCE

I sweep through full, yet empty rooms,
and crave the sunshine of your face.
I trod the paths I've walked with you
and long for even just a trace... of you.

I move my form from place to place
while silent cries surge from within.
I bring myself from here to there
and fill my days with righteous tasks.

My arms reach out across the lake,
as if sheer will could pull you back,
While lapping waters bring with them
sweet treasures held in memory.

Yet all the while, the love from you
engulfs my heart, my soul, my mind,
and smoothes the darkness of the night,
to help my sleepy eyes to close.

As true as etchings boldly drawn,
each plane of you remains in sight,
and I awake and find you still
within the confines of myself.

Chapter 19

"What lies behind us and what lies
before us are tiny matters to what
lies within us."
Ralph Waldo Emerson

Sometimes it seems like the agony that accompanies grief simply won't go away. All the energy of wanting it to go just isn't enough to make it happen. Coming out of sadness is hard enough, but coming out from under despair when it throws its cloak over you, is an even more difficult task. Wanting something to change or be different while knowing you can't make it so by sheer will, is very frustrating.

Even with all the good and helpful advice in the world, going through any kind of grief is not easy. Anyone who has ever dealt with grief and tried to make some sense out of it knows that full well. There are times when no amount of faith or praying seems to get you anywhere. There are times when you want to punch something, or scream and shout to the heavens in anger and frustration. There are times when everything seems so futile. There seems to be no kind of help, no answers. There is only despair, and you feel as if you're living in the middle of it.

Despair seems to come in all shades of gray, from the deepest darkest gray, when you are down in the depths, to the heavy clouds of gray that seem to hang over you as you go about your day. Despair, often a familiar companion when you are grieving, can eat away at your heart. I try to steer clear of residing with it, even though its darkness can be inviting at times. Sometimes there is a comfort in curling up in the darkness with despair as your companion. It feels like a shelter from an even more unbearable pain in the light.

The unhealthy thing about despair is that it gives up on hope. It blots out the sun and makes you think that those sad gray clouds will stay over you forever. It's reminiscent of that feeling you get after days and days of rain, when you try to remember what the sun looks like, or how warm it feels in a bold blue sky. Because it often comes upon you uninvited, there are times when it's hard to find the strength to fight it.

One Sunday, during a particularly grievous time, I was in church, wrapped in a gray sadness. We were singing a baptismal hymn with a line that tugged at my heart. It read, "Should you find someone to share your time, and you join your hearts as one, I'll be there to make your verses rhyme, from dusk till rising sun". I was suddenly overcome with emotion by the words. I looked to my left and saw a man and woman reach for each other's hand, smile, and look at each other knowingly. At that point, I could no longer hold back my tears.

Feeling myself on the verge of losing my composure and breaking down completely, I got up and walked out of the church. I got into my car, and with tears rolling down my cheeks, drove away. I drove around for a while until my mind began to settle down. Observing such love and happiness in a time of despair, had the ability to break open my fragile heart. Just as it's hard to recall a happy time while residing in sorrow, it is equally hard to observe the happiness of others when you are in that state of mind.

As I began to talk to myself and try to attain some measure of peace, I thought about the unmistakable happiness of the couple I had observed. I found as I did so, that I was filled with a sense of joy over their obvious love for each other. They had met at a convention for their mutual profession, she from the East coast and he from the West coast. They had fallen in love with each other and, eventually, he had relocated to be with her. Second marriage for both of them, they had married each other on a beach in Hawaii. How perfect! The very first time I saw them together, I was aware of how much they loved and cherished each other.

It was difficult for me to observe the obvious love they felt for each other, because I knew from experience, exactly how that felt. I had been there, and it was hard for me to be reminded of it during a time of such sadness. I drove around and thought about our good fortune--those of us who have experienced the blessing that comes from loving and being loved back. My mood began a transformation into one of thankfulness. We were some of the lucky ones. It was good to be reminded that life is about both sadness and joy. Beautiful memories remind us of joy, just like having flowers in the winter remind us of the spring.

BENEATH MY HEART

Shreds of strangled sobs,
residue of stifled cries,
all emotion running wild,
crashing into shouting fears.

Strains of shredded sanity
fight to grasp life's molding,
reach to keep it firmly bound,
securing dread's sharp edges.

Gasping, just to breath the air,
littered fine with hurt's debris,
filtering traumas slowly through,
hope against hope's promise,
seeks to find pain's refuge.

Screaming, drowning, sorrow's fate
knows its truth in me.
Memories of a hundred splinters
echo lonely down through time.

Excruciating, stabbing pain
cascades life's waterfall,
spilling dregs of time's remorse
winging on the frozen breeze.

Deeper, nearer to my core
drives this wedge of ceaseless pain.
Heavens comfort gone amiss,
forsaking me again.

Shattered pieces of my heart
are all that now remain.
Sawdust, blown on morning winds,
softly fall upon my shell.

Chapter 20

"Life is not a 'brief candle'. It is a splendid
torch that I want to make burn as brightly as
possible before handing it on to future generations."
George Bernard Shaw

I have a list on my counter this morning, a list of things
to do and people I should call. My cupboard is bare, and I
know I must finally give in and do the grocery shopping
that I've put off for so long. Yet, it's bitterly cold outdoors
and comfortably warm in my house. What I really feel like
doing is just sitting down and writing, so that's probably
what I'll do. I like to follow my instincts and move in
directions that feel right to me. My youngest son, Brian,
seems to imitate that trait at times. Maybe it's because he
seemed to grow up quicker than the rest of my children
and understands about the brevity of life.

Brian has experienced first hand, the pain and sorrow
of losing loved ones to death. Most of us don't have to
deal with death at a young age, but he has had to deal
with it often in the ten years between 7 and 17 years of
age. The first experience I ever had with death was when
my grandmother died. At 17, I don't remember her death
seeming very traumatic. The only thing that stands out in
my mind is the fact that I had to come home from college
for her funeral.

Brian was only a little guy when his father died. Being
seven years old makes it difficult to comprehend what it

means when you ask your mom why your dad had to die, and she hasn't got all the answers. I think one thing I realized about talking to a child about death is that although we don't come anywhere near to having all the answers, we have to tell them something that rings true.

Telling a child that his dad has gone off on a journey, or is up in heaven, or any of the other instances of appeasement we might think will protect them from hurt, really doesn't work. I simply told him what I believed in my heart. I said, "I don't know why people we love have to die and leave us sad from missing them. I wish I did. I don't have all the answers but I'd like to believe that they have gone to a wonderful place where they are happy. So, even though we will miss them, we know that they're alright."

On the day David died, Brian had arrived home from school right after I'd checked his pulse and realized he was gone. I sent Brian to the store with a friend, never telling him at that point that his dad was dead. David's body was still seated in his recliner, covered with his many blankets. With his eyes closed, he looked like he was sleeping. I had to wait for the doctor to arrive and pronounce him dead before the undertaker could come and take him away. To me, it didn't seem like the appropriate time to let him know his dad had died.

Later, when Brian came back from the store, everything had been taken care of. David was gone from his usual spot in the living room. It was then that I told him his dad had died. I can still remember his small form, perched on the stacked pillows on the recliner, arms folded across his chest, looking at me angrily.

Some time later we talked about that day, and he told me that he had been angry because he hadn't had a chance to say "Good-bye". I apologized, explaining that my only concern at the time was that he not be traumatized by the fact that his father was lying dead in the living room. I told him that, as a parent, I had only done what I perceived to be best for him at the time. After listening to him, I realized that I had been wrong in the way I'd handled it. He had needed some kind of closure even though he was a small boy.

A few years after David's death, my brother drowned. He had been a favorite of Brian's. Once again we sat talking, this time at the end of the dock at the lake where we now lived. It had been our healing place when we began coming there after his dad's death. I don't remember my exact words at that time. I do know that Brian, because of his poignant experience four years earlier, had some kind of an ineffable understanding of what was going on. The two of us sat close together on the dock for a long time, talking about the mystery and the complexity of death.

Accepting that death is one of the inevitabilities of life is something most of us don't do in our early years, but Brian accepted it at a very young age because he had come face to face with death and loss more than once. Most of us aren't comfortable thinking or talking about it. It's one of those things we put off. Some of us never think about it at all, until we are faced with it.

Brian went on to lose his beloved godmother a few years later. This time there was a quiet acceptance of his loss. One day, shortly after her death, I found an unusual sight among the various things my son and his friends would leave on the porch. Most summer days were spent snorkeling, swimming, catching frogs and turtles, or playing board games, and the items left on the porch usually attested to those pass-times.

This time, on the coffee table, next to the Trivial Pursuit game, was a Bible and a prayer book. Brian's answer to my question about what they were doing was simply, "We were having a religious discussion." Because this was not the normal activity of a bunch of 14 and 15 year old boys, I was astounded. Still, I couldn't help but think that it was a good thing, this discussion they had had. I suspect that it came about partly because of what had happened in Brian's life.

When Walt was dying, he was in the hospital for four days before he died. Most of us find it difficult to see a loved one in a hospital situation where they are compromised, and totally at the mercy of their infirmity. Brian was no exception and didn't want to go and see Walt, but he asked me if I would bring him the small wooden Dutch cradle cross he had been given at his baptism. I did. I placed it in Walt's hand. When he died a few days later, it was still clutched in his hand, in spite of nurses and doctors moving him around while seeing to his needs. I found it overwhelmingly comforting, this connection between my youngest son and a father that he'd spent the last ten years with.

Shortly after Walt died, Brian started college. He chose to commute and go to school close to home, even though he'd been accepted at a college out of state that he had wanted to go to. It was a great comfort to me to have him around after Walt's death.

Once, while he and I were floating around in the lake, the summer after he'd graduated from college, he asked me why everyone says that after you graduate you have to get a 'real' job. I've never said that, because I feel it's the one time in your life that you're free to do whatever you please, and I told him so. We live in a country where the sky is the limit when it comes to where you want to go, and what you want to do in your life. As long as you can support and take care of yourself, why not experience life while you're not responsible for anyone but yourself.

Brian went off to live on the Pacific coast, far away from me, a few years after he graduated. He moved away from the town he grew up in and left an empty space in my house. It's always hardest when the last child moves away. When he was living at home, he'd sometimes knock on my bedroom door in the early hours of the morning, after working late as a bartender, and ask if he could sing me a new song he'd written. He had become an accomplished guitar player and singer, basically self-taught. I never minded being woken up, in spite of the hour, because I knew that his time at home would soon come to and end and I'd be wishing I could have it back.

I think that this son of mine, in his acceptance of the inevitability of death at an early age, has more insight into such things than most young people do. I have a feeling that he may, somewhere in his life, have something to offer others from it. It might have something to do with some kind of work or profession, or maybe he'll just be there for another person in their time of need, equipped with a special understanding gained from his own experiences with loss.

LITTLE WISHES

I wish that time and life would pause
And in that space, that it would cause
A respite in your day.

I wish that arms could hold you near
And so dispel all trace of fear,
Transferring waves of peace.

I wish your heart could open wide
And in its confines find inside,
Those mountain peaks of joy.

I wish cascades of pure delight
Would rain on you and drown your plight,
Just drenching you in love.

I wish life's sorrows would abate
And bid you never hesitate
To welcome in 'the gift'.

Chapter 21

"Hope is the thing with feathers that
perches in the soul and sings the tune
without the words and never stops at all."
Emily Dickinson

Within the confines of life's most difficult experiences
there are so many lessons to be learned. Without the
experiences of sorrow, sadness, trauma, and adversity, how
would we find our greatest strength or realize our highest
potential? It is only on the other side of grief--that place
where we gulp great breaths of clear fresh air--that we
become aware of the growth we have attained. I look back
at where I was before I traveled that road, and I'm amazed
at the distance I've come.

My husband, David, died at age 45 and my husband,
Walt, at age 51. Each experience was different; each man
was different in the way he handled illness and the prospect
of death. When I knew that Walt was terminally ill, I was
aware of how much my reserves of strength and knowledge
of the process would help me through it. Knowing that I
would survive the grieving that would follow his death, was
registered somewhere in my subconscious. When Walt was
dying, my conscious mind didn't want to believe it would
ever happen. Afterward, when I knew it all to be so true, I
felt like no one would ever come along that could take his
place, or bring me such happiness, again.

No one ever takes the place of another. I've come to know that. Ultimately, each person remains in that special circle of love reserved for them alone. Fortunately, the human heart has an infinite capacity to love, and love again it will, if given the chance.

Each experience of loving has its own panorama of remembered treasures, and that is often a cloak of comfort for those who mourn. Sometimes though, it's too painful to remember the happy times after a loved one is gone. After Walt died, I sometimes found it especially hard to even think of him at all. I sent the memory off to a safe place when I found that its presence brought me too much pain.

I executed a mental exercise that I called "putting it on the shelf". Doing that wasn't like trying to avoid it altogether. Trying to avoid the memories altogether, caused them to come crashing down around me the moment my emotional stability was compromised. When I promised myself that I could take them down off the shelf any time I wished, I gave myself an alternative. The memories were still there, safely waiting for a time when I could handle them. It felt better, having them in a place of safekeeping, rather than trying to extinguish them from my mind altogether.

In my mind, I would picture a shelf in back of me, where I could place the memories when they were too painful. I would mentally put them up there, promising myself that I could take them down any time I wanted to. Sometimes, when I would test taking them down again, I had to put them back. When I finally felt that it was safe to remember, I took them down from the shelf. Eventually, when enough time had passed, I could allow them to tumble down at will. It takes time, but the day finally comes when a reminder of someone who has gone from your sight, only causes a small catch in your breathing and no longer makes you feel that it has completely taken away your ability to breathe at all.

When I allowed my heart to grieve and experience the physical loss, I traveled through my pain. It was only in going there, to the sorrow that was housed in my core, that I was able to put myself back together and renew my spirit. In allowing myself to break apart like tiny pieces of shattered glass, I gave myself permission to reside within the ache of my wounded heart, and permission to put myself back together when I was done.

There is no shame in being wounded. There is no need to be forgiven for falling apart, nor is there any need to have to explain why you have done so. No apology is necessary for spending time with grief. In fact, it is in not going there that more harm is done to hearts that have already been compromised by loss.

After healing, as if emerging from a coma, I began to experience life in its myriad aspects once again, happily taking in all that was good. How easy it had been to forget how fulfilling life can be, when sadness was my daily companion. I'd forgotten about all the joy and delight that can be found in all there is to see and do. I'd forgotten how wonderful it is to wake up and feel happy.

Life doesn't deserve to be wasted. It asks to be lived. Our loved ones, who have gone before us, wouldn't want us to stagnate and miss out on all life has to offer. They would want us to live life to its fullest.

I have a framed saying by Oliver Wendell Holmes, which was read at my mom's funeral service. It says, "I find the great thing in this world is not so much where we stand, as in what direction we are moving: to reach the port of Heaven, we must sail sometimes with the wind and sometimes against it, but we must sail and not drift, nor lie at anchor."

მ

ON MY SHELF

There's a man upon my shelf
as fine as he can be.
There's a man upon my shelf,
whose heart belongs to me.
As he sits, I dream of him
Just slightly, so to keep
my heart intact,
my mind at ease,
myself from falling deep into the pit.

There's a place so deep inside
where I can keep him safe.
There's a reason he has said
for me to hold his place.
So as I go along my way,
I sometimes take him down
and hold him tight--
my calm to bring
when things aren't going right within myself.

Most the time, I leave him there,
not even breathe his name.
Then sometimes I hide from him,
so I won't go insane.
On I go about my life,
pretending I am free,

without his smile,
without his laugh,
without his eyes on me, forever mine.

There's a man upon my shelf.
I love him faithfully.
For that man upon my shelf
is truly life to me.
As he sits, I wait for him,
so patient, for I long
to be his own
and take him in
and give the life I've shown belongs to him.

Chapter 22

"The grand essentials in life are,
something to do, something to
love, and something to hope for."
Allan K. Chalmers

It's good to know during those times when we struggle with sorrow, what to do for ourselves to accomplish the task of bringing our hearts back to their home of residence. I have always had a wide variety of interests, and I mentally run down the list of things I can immerse myself in when I am beset by an event or situation that brings on sadness.

I have a close friend who left her job a few years back because the atmosphere at her job became so unhealthy. She loved her work as a nurse and had done it all of her life, yet she knew enough about herself to realize that she had to leave if she was to be happy. On the day she left, she was not only sad about leaving some of the people she worked with, but she was afraid she might never work in her field again.

She told me on that day after she'd left work, she went to the store and bought pre-cooked food and canned vegetables, something completely foreign for her to do. She informed her husband that since she would probably be residing in bed for a good part of the next few days, these items would be for his meals. After going to the library and taking out a few books to read, she went home to bed, to nurture herself, as she put it. She told me that she knew what to do for herself in times of sadness or grief, and spending time in bed while reading books helped her to do the nurturing necessary to bring her back to a place where she was all right again.

When my husband, Walt, was going through chemotherapy, he usually felt very sick to his stomach the next day after his treatment; but he would go to work anyway. When his doctor asked him why he didn't stay home, he replied, "I could feel just as lousy at home as at work, but at work, there is always a chance of meeting up with a customer who has a bigger problem to deal with than I do. Then it's easy to forget about my little problems."

One of the most important pieces of advice I can give about grieving is that it's important to surround yourself with friends and family, people who care. If I go somewhere and talk with someone who cares about me, or if I go and do something that shows I care about someone else, it's amazing how easy it is to forget about my own problems for a while. When I do volunteer or charity work, if I am sad, just the act of helping someone else makes me feel better.

Even the simple task of making something for someone else works for me--be it baked goods or handmade treasures. The act of writing a long overdue letter to an older person who looks forward to mail, or a visit to a shut-in, does wonders for my state of mind. Eventually, when I find myself really involved in something, I forget about myself for a while and usually find myself enjoying what I'm doing.

I got through the difficult times in my life by paying attention to what made me feel better. I immersed myself in the kind of work that I've always loved. I crocheted, knitted, sewed, and painted. I did anything that could involve me so thoroughly, that I didn't really have to think about what I was doing. At the same time, I was also occupying myself to the point of becoming peaceful. I could lose myself in doing things I loved to do, tasks that brought me pleasure and even find to my surprise that hours had passed without feeling my sadness.

After I was divorced and became a single parent, I often felt sad and lonely. There wasn't a lot of opportunity to go out on my own without my children. However, since I believed that my being happy was a boon to my children, I made sure that I involved myself in things that were good for me and helped me stay centered. I had two very good friends who I kept constant company with. We went to the same church, bowled in the same bowling league, and belonged to the same Junior Women's Club. They were both very special friends, always there when I needed them.

One of my friends was also divorced, like me, and the other one's husband very often couldn't get away from his busy job, so we became a familiar threesome at get-togethers. Most people came as couples to the social functions, but it never stopped the three of us from going together. Once we went to a dance that was a huge fundraiser and got to listen to the band and socialize, while playing hostess and selling raffle tickets. Another time we went on a hayride together and laughed ourselves silly the whole time.

My husband David and I belonged to a club where for many years we both went on Friday nights to be with friends and to play darts. Even after he didn't feel up to going, I would still go. He insisted, and he was right to do so. The time I spent out was invaluable to me, and when I came home, he was happy to hear about everyone and about who had won the dart games. It was good for both of us.

The summer before he died, Walt had a visiting nurse three times a week, in the morning. I would take the opportunity to go out to breakfast with my two summer friends at the lake. One of my friends also had the visiting nurse for her husband. Every week, we looked forward to our couple of hours of freedom during those three mornings. Our perspective would change, and we would go back renewed, ready for the rest of the day with our husbands. I think we visited and checked out almost every breakfast spot in the surrounding area that summer!

It's easy to become depressed when someone is ill if you don't take yourself out of the picture once in a while. It only takes a little time away to restore the equilibrium needed to carry on and take care. I advocate it to any and all caregivers.

ஃ

OF SORROW AND SUCH

Of sorrow, I have known its depths and suffered its extent.
Of sadness, I have felt its weight, throughout my heart and soul.

Of numbness, I am conscious, each cell its touch recalls.
Each fiber of my being, still feels its heavy load.

Of respite, I am certain, my weighty heart responds,
With clear, sweet bells of calmness and gulps of memory's store.

Of joy, I am reminded, its heady fragrance trails
So sweetly in my confines and circles round my heart.

With you, I am surrounded, your love still sweeps me in,
And your abiding presence resides inside me still.

Go surely on your way, my Love, with sorrow left behind,
Still quietly accepting this love I send with you.

Chapter 23

"The essence of all spiritual life is your emotion, your attitude toward others. Once you have sincere motivation, all the rest will follow."
The Dalai Lama, The Path to Tranquility

For a long time after Walt died of AIDS, I had this feeling that there was something I was supposed to do in that area. I tried to think of a way to help in some capacity, possibly with a volunteer job. I wanted the tragic circumstances of his death to mean something, and I wanted to be the one to make it meaningful.

When I first thought about it, I think it was too soon after his death, and I had not really gotten over my grieving. Later, when I thought of it again, I was trying to find a different kind of fulfillment for myself and probably couldn't have devoted myself to anything connected with people having AIDS. Then one day I heard a broadcast on PBS about a home for AIDS patients in a place close by and I got excited about the possibility of maybe doing something there. Still, I wasn't quite ready. There may have been some hidden fears going on inside me about being involved with people with AIDS. The idea of watching anyone waste away from the disease was coupled with a poignant memory of watching Walt deteriorate from it.

Six years after Walt's death, a chance meeting came about after a World Day of Prayer service at the church in the town Walter grew up in. As my cousin and I made our way down the stairs for coffee afterward, we passed a neat looking older woman, standing just inside the doorway. She was lovely in her countenance, with a beautiful shawl wrapped around her shoulders. My cousin greeted her saying, "Isn't this funny, I just saw you yesterday at work, and now I see you again, here tonight." She introduced me to the woman, who she said worked in her building, as a volunteer for AIDS Project Hartford. I was astounded. The words AIDS and volunteer had quickened my heartbeat.

Excitedly, I told the woman that I'd always wanted to do some volunteer work with AIDS because my husband had died of it. It turned out that she had known my husband! She told me that AIDS Project Hartford was badly in need of someone to help as a receptionist right away. I quickly volunteered for the job. When she said that God must have sent me, there was no doubt in my mind about it.

Previous to our meeting I had heard an ad on the radio about a week before about AIDS Project Hartford. Something inside of me knew I should get involved, although I wasn't sure how to go about it. Even though I felt I should make a call, I was reticent to do so. My perfect opportunity appeared before me because the 'knowing I was supposed to do it' was within me, and I had put it out there. I was overwhelmed once again by the way good things happen in our lives, with a plan much better than I could have thought up myself.

I talked with the woman and told her that I knew quite a bit about AIDS as I had spent many years doing research, while trying to find out everything I could to help my husband with the disease. I told her I had even done some writing about it. Subsequently, in the same year that I started my volunteer job at APH, I was asked to give a speech at a service on Dec.1st, World AIDS Day. It was also Walt's birthday. My speech was about him and about dealing with the disease and his death.

As I've previously stated, to find fulfillment, it helps to step outside yourself, and it's easier to be happy when you're doing something to help others. It sounds simple, but it means far more than that. It's about making a meaningful difference. Little acts of kindness have a way of becoming cumulative. Doing something for someone else brings immense joy and satisfaction back to you. For me, volunteering at APH was about making Walt's life and death more meaningful by helping the HIV/AIDS community and those working in it.

AIDS Project Hartford, Inc. is a non-profit organization, which provides educational and support services to people affected by HIV/AIDS, regardless of age, race, religion, ethnic origin, gender, sexual orientation, or financial circumstances. It was founded by a committed core of volunteers in 1985. During the past two decades, the agency's programs have adapted to meet the needs of people affected by HIV/AIDS, retaining its commitment to providing the best services to them. It relies heavily on the generosity of its supporters in the community.

I MET YOU TODAY

I met with your soul today
while on its way through life.
It intertwined with mine.

I brushed by your heart today
while on my way to share
a joy beyond belief.

I found you again my Love,
so deeply etched in me
that boundaries had no place.

I sang from within myself
as I passed through your form,
emerging sorrow-free.

I won back my faith today,
so mirrored in your eyes,
my life became renewed.

I lay in your arms today
and heard you say my name--
a whisper in your sleep.

With you I set sail today
to places yet to be,
for now, still undefined.

I met you again today
the same, yet all complete,
my faith in what will be.

Chapter 24

"When you cease to dream
you cease to live."
Malcolm S. Forbes

On a sunny March morning, when there was still snow on the ground, and a thin layer of ice on the lake, I sat on my lower deck and contemplated the ebb and flow of my life. The ice was beginning to melt, and channels of water were starting to wind their way into the white blanket that was covering the lake's expanse. The birds were making a lot of noise, already aware that spring was on its way.

I sat there on my weather-worn glider bench, the one I never seemed to get around to putting away before the winter set in. It was warm in the corner, on my bench, where I was sheltered from the wind. I shed my big, bulky, winter sweater and sat there in my long sleeve shirt, my face turned upward toward the sun, basking in its warmth.

I felt a little sad, sitting there alone on my bench. Sometimes, when I am sad and wistful, even the brilliance of the morning sun shining on the lake can't diminish those feelings. Knowing that I am fortunate to live in a place of such beauty, doesn't always help me out. Sadness comes over me unbidden at times when I least expect it, or when my defenses are down. Heaven must know me well, for each and every time I have to ask for help.

It was that kind of a morning for me, sitting there in the sunshine. I tried to renew my faith, as I sat there and took in the view. I heard John Denver singing the words, "Sunshine on my shoulder makes me happy. Sunshine in my eyes can make me cry. Sunshine on the waters looks so lovely. Sunshine almost always makes me high." His words touched that place inside me where the sunshine made me happy too, but also made me cry.

I wonder sometimes, when I read books about living in the 'now' and staying positive, who achieves this desirable state of mind on a permanent basis? I'm so proud of myself when I can achieve this state of being for even a few minutes, but I'm still disconcerted by the fact that I can't hold onto it for very long.

All the stories of my life and the people I've loved who've come and gone make for a colorful scenario. If someone had told me when I was young that by the time I was in my 60's, I would have gone through so many different relationships and experiences, I wouldn't have believed it. That's because I always thought that I would simply fall in love with someone who fell in love with me. Then we would get married, and be together forever. We'd have children who were a part of the love we had for each other, and we'd spend our lives raising them together.

I've managed to survive the sorrows of all those years and in spite of its twists and turns, retain the unshakable belief that life has truly been good to me. In all of my years of relationships, no one has ever beaten or abused me. No one has ever really been mean to me. I have had hard times, and I have had good times. I have had many satisfying moments in raising my children and endured the trials and tribulations of being a parent. I've always been able to keep a roof over their heads, and I've always been able to feed them-- surviving for a while with the blessing of food stamps, when we were very poor. We made it through it all, and we did it with lots of love and laughter along the way. The result is five amazingly wonderful human beings.

I have also been lucky enough to be able to do the kind of work I love. Ever since I was eight years old, I have been sewing. I love to sew. I love the creative part and the satisfaction I feel when the job is done. I love sewing for other people, making them happy by doing so, and making a living at the same time. Sewing has not only helped to support us, but it has also helped to support my pride in myself.

Life for me has been one of constant change, but I think change is a good thing. Even though we fight it at times, often in retrospect, we recognize its value. The most significant changes in our lives seem to come about when we are open and receptive to the good that can enter, if we let it. One of the most important things I have learned is to not struggle so, trying to figure out the 'why' of things. Sometimes, it's better to just let it all go and wait.

I still want it all. I don't want to accept anything less. I don't want to just go along, living from day to day, as if it were just something to get through. I want to feel so alive when I wake up and know that the possibilities of the day in front of me are endless. I want to explore and experience them all.

NEVER GONE

All time stands still without you.
My shape awaits your form.
My longing cannot be assuaged,
Till vacant eyes can take you in.

My memory retains you.
My heart claws at your door.
Please let me in so I can stay
Safe in a corner of your soul.

The sun shines warm upon me.
The birds their song expend.
Why don't you know my empty arms
Are aching for the feel of you?

All of yourself you gave me,
A love so pure--apart
From fear or pain or unbelief
In all there is that's really true.

For always I am with you
And you are here with me,
Just soulmates on the wings of time--
Two hearts inside one heart we are.

Chapter 25

"We cannot do great things on this
earth, only small things with great love."
Mother Theresa

My sister, Fran, marches to the beat of a different drummer-- always has, always will. Sometimes I even march along with her. It's fun to veer off my normal path and do that. We have lived very different lives, she and I, but I respect who she is and her paths of choice, as she does mine. The best part about my sister and I is that we speak the same language. No interpretation is necessary.

Growing up with her was like having a best friend living with me. We are fourteen months apart. As children, my mother often dressed us in matching outfits, and we looked so much alike that many people took us for twins! When we were growing up we were close-- talking, laughing, and confiding in each other. We told my mother we would always be that way. She said when we grew up and went our separate ways it wouldn't be like that any more. We swore it would. To this day it still is.

People marvel at how close we are, even after years of each raising five children in two entirely different manners. The bond remains the same after many years of living apart and only seeing each other now and then. We always retained the same loyalty to each other. Through trial and tribulation, husbands that came and went, and changes that could never have been anticipated when we were growing up, we still remained close.

It isn't that we always agree on everything, but we never fight about differences, never become angry at each other over disagreements. When I tell people that this is the kind of relationship I have with my sister, they are incredulous. I, who have always taken this relationship for granted, am surprised that more sisters don't share this kind of bond.

I'm not really sure why it is that we share this closeness. I only know that when I'm happy, my sister Fran is happy for me, and when I'm sad she shares my sorrow and is there to comfort me. I don't know how I would have survived some of the grief in my life without her steadfast love to support me. For me, she is like a bulwark in a storm. To share my happiness with her only brings more laughter and delight to the situation. To bring her my pain or sadness makes my load lighter because she automatically shoulders half the burden.

It is beyond me how she ever puts up with my incessant chatter, about anything that's bothering me, or something that makes my heart sing. Even more incredible is the fact that she always remains understanding and nonjudgmental. She listens quietly and only offers advice when it is called for. Her wisdom in knowing when that is strikes me as even more extraordinary.

I am the older sister, and I used to lord that over her throughout our growing up years. I think she always looked up to me, and because of that, would do anything for me. When my mother got angry and yelled at me, Fran cried.

I could make her do almost anything just by threatening to tickle her. She was extremely ticklish while I, on the other hand, was not. We used to do the dishes together every night, singing songs from my mother's song sheet that was propped up behind the faucets. If I didn't want to be the drier (I liked washing better), I could get her to change with me even though it wasn't my turn, simply by tickling her!

She has been, among other things-- a mother, a hippie, a farmer, a seeker, and a journeyman on the road of life. I'm pretty sure she hasn't finished yet although she's slowed down a bit as she's gotten older. We do that. I think we mellow as we get into those later years. A month after our mother died, Fran broke her leg and was laid up for quite a while. She says she thinks maybe it was a sign that she needed to slow down and reassess herself and her life at that point. Because it followed so soon after my mom's death, it served as a very reflective time for her.

Everyone should have a soul mate like the one I have in my sister, Fran. To be understood and admired for who you are in spite of your flaws has got to be the best kind of a relationship to have. My sister and I love and respect each other. We never tire of talking and laughing. Sometimes we go over and over something until it's beaten to death. Fran's husband shakes his head and refuses to find anything funny in the subject matter that has sent us off into bouts of laughter, bringing tears to our eyes.

Fran came back to the East coast to stay when my mother became ill a few years ago. The first night we slept together in my big king size bed. We talked and laughed into the early morning. My son, Brian, upon hearing us still laughing at three o'clock in the morning, stuck his head in my bedroom door and said, "I thought I told you two kids to go to sleep!" Memories of our parents saying that to us when we were young enveloped us and sent us into peals of laughter.

It's hard to believe sometimes, that Fran and I have spent most of our lives away from each other, reuniting only during family occasions and vacations. It's also hard to believe that, in spite of hardly ever seeing each other over the years of raising our kids, we picked right up where we left off, now that they are all grown up. It was as if no time has passed in between. Having Fran nearby for those years after our mom died was a treat. There was always much to talk about. There was always something I wanted to share with her. I miss that now that she's moved on.

I wish for everyone a sister like mine, a sister who gives them the kind of love my sister gives me. There cannot be a more satisfying relationship than that. We were two girls who grew into women, yet kept the same closeness we had always shared. We are two women who, although battered about by life's storms, have survived to become stronger and wiser, never losing the bond we shared at the start. We are two women who can count on each other's support through thick and thin. I love my sister Fran, with all my heart.

TWO GIFTS

A gift was given long ago,
the precious power to love.
The heart awaits the second gift,
someone to love, be worthy of.

The tired heart impatient grows--
knows hunger, even thirst,
Grows faithless in its haste to give
the second gift, the first.

And restlessly it does not heed
a small voice in the air
that whispers down, "Your need for love,
God knows before it's ever there."

Love steals upon you quietly
bourne on the wings of Spring
or softly in the fall of leaves--
an ever joyful ring.

For you may never see it come
although a thousand eyes you bear.
It pours into your very soul
'til suddenly you feel it there.

Forever lasts the disbelief...
this precious gift was given free.
And all the love I bring to you
and give you, never seems to be
enough to ever show my thanks.
So great the gift, so small my fee.

Chapter 26

"The greatest of the practiced arts
is to live life deeply, fully."
Karen Burton Mains

It was five days before Walt died, and I was still hoping it wouldn't happen. We were expecting our lawyer to come by so that Walt could sign some papers. At that moment his bowels let go, and I was suddenly faced with the job of cleaning him up and making him presentable before she arrived. She was an old friend and, although I knew she understood about the odor that permeated the room, I still felt the need to apologize.

There was very little dignity left for my husband at that point. Once he would have been totally humiliated to be found in such a compromising position, but on that day he was just a shell of the man he had once been and dignity had no say. There was little that mattered enough for him to bother being upset about, and I couldn't blame him. We had come to a place where the quality of life was at its lowest. I knew I'd have to give in to the inevitable truth that he would leave me soon.

I was reminded of that day as I listened to the caseworkers at AIDS Project Hartford express their grief over the clients they had lost to AIDS. Someone had come to talk about grieving, and to show us a meaningful video about loss and how to handle it. The music was soothing, the scenery showing the change of seasons, comparing it expertly with our lives. It was done beautifully. The words of hope that were spoken throughout the presentation were inspirational to us all.

What happened to everyone during the video was that we all came in touch with our own grief. Most of these caseworkers, all such caring individuals, had had multiple losses. Working with people who have HIV/AIDS had brought them in touch with death often. But more than that, the video reminded us all of our own personal losses, our family, our loved ones and our friends

Almost everyone seemed to experience an emotional release. Some hadn't yet cried or truly grieved over the losses they had had to deal with in the past. Others still felt guilty about feelings they had that made them want to distance themselves from the pain.

It was a cleansing experience, that brief time in the darkened room, watching the soothing video. It served to bring things out in all of us that we hadn't dealt with. I was no exception. Hearing people talk about AIDS patients, and the debilitating situations they find themselves in when their whole system becomes compromised, forced me to remember some things I'd tried to forget.

There is no need to dwell on such things, and it's not good to let the images haunt us, but reminders of them serve to keep us from becoming complacent. It pays now and then, to be made aware of how fragile life really is.

We all became painfully aware of how fragile life is, when one of the employees at Aids Project Hartford died, at the age of 50. He was a great guy who was loved by everyone. Living with AIDS means you constantly have to be careful about infections and getting sick, because your immune system is so compromised. One day he was with us, looking happy and healthy, and the next day he was in the hospital, never to return.

It affected everyone in the office, all those people who, daily, came face to face with people who were living with HIV/AIDS. The memorial service for this man was overflowing with people who had known him and would miss him sorely. It was a very emotional gathering. One of the case workers had a poem for the ceremony, about the man and his passing. Because she was too emotional to read it, her husband read it for her.

God looked around his garden
And found an empty space.
Then he looked upon the earth
And saw your weary face.

He knew of all your suffering.
He knew of all your pain.
He knew that you would soon be needing,
Shelter from the rain.

He knew the road was far too long,
The hills too hard and steep,
So then he closed your clear blue eyes
And let you go to sleep.

Then He put his arms around you,
And laid you down to rest.
God's garden must be beautiful
for He only takes the best.

Dear Lord, please pick a flower
The nicest one you see,
And place it close to Larry's heart...
He'll know that it's from me.

AIDS Project Hartford opened a drop-in-center recently and I found myself offering to help out there also. One morning a week, I go there and sit at the desk where people come in. They are all clients of the Ryan White program, people with HIV/AIDS.

The federal Ryan White Comprehensive AIDS Resources Emergency (CARE) Act was originally enacted on August 18, 1990. The CARE Act is named for Ryan White, an 18 year old Indiana teenager with hemophilia who died of AIDS in 1990. The primary goal of the CARE Act, which is made up of five program areas know as "titles", is to improve the quality and availability of care for individuals and families affected by HIV disease.

The clients go to the drop-in-center to meet with their case managers, have a meal, relax in the TV room, or take advantage of the many programs offered there for their benefit. I go there to answer the phone, but talking to the people who go there is my favorite part. I like them all and it pleases me to think they might like me as well.

Usually I'm knitting a prayer shawl, and usually someone asks me what I'm knitting. It's a good conversation starter. So, I tell them about the prayer shawl ministry which is a ministry of giving. It's widespread and its purpose is to give comfort and consolation to those who have suffered a loss or who are ill, but it's equally as gratifying to be the person who makes and gives the shawl and sends prayers with it.

I go to that drop-in-center once every week to renew my own spirit, for when I go there, my perspective changes.

I leave my beautiful lake and my cozy home and I go to a place 50 minutes away to spend time with people who remind me how fortunate I am. I've been in places of despair before, I've been afraid before and I've felt alone at times in my life. I go there with my knitting, and always feel at peace when I sit at my desk in the lobby, accomplishing many things.

A DWELLING PLACE

If I could hear your voice, I'd open my mouth
and draw it in, saving its beautiful resonance
to envelope and console me when I ached for you.

If I could experience your laughter,
I'd catch it in its flight, and place it on my tongue,
to taste its sweetness once again.

If I could harness your thoughts,
I'd fold them up, tuck them into my pocket,
and carry them securely against me.

If I could capture your smile
I'd paste it behind my eyes.

If I could feel your breath on my face as I slept
I'd sleep in heaven's clouds.

If I could own the warmth of your skin when you awoke,
I'd rub it gently over mine.

If I could feel what you feel,
I'd make it a roof to shelter my secret longings.

If you went down to the depths,
I'd hold you until you knew joy again.
I would cover you in love,
drawing it up from the deepest part of me,
and wrap it tightly around your heart.

I would stay there with you
until you climbed once more to the highest peak,
swung on the end of a rainbow,
lay in the curve of the crescent moon,
and lived out eternity with me.

Chapter 27

"The world breaks everyone and afterward
many are stronger at the broken parts."
Ernest Hemingway

When I look back on the times in my life when I have
mourned, I realize that they have also been some of the
most productive times of my life, as far as my own personal
growth. What happened was that they became places where
I learned far more about myself than I'd known before.

So often, I felt helpless and completely out of control,
no longer in charge. As human beings, we are creatures
who like to think we are in charge of things. We might
be in charge of ourselves, but there are forces far beyond
our control that can blow us off our course, even as we are
commending ourselves for doing well. At such times, we
are reminded that life is littered with changes and fraught
with obstacles.

Trying to keep positive when life feels like it's crashing
down around you, is an extremely difficult task. Sometimes,
in the direst of circumstances, I have found a reserve of
strength I didn't even know I possessed. Within that
reserve, I remember that I possess all the tools to make
myself happy, if I make use of them. Thinking positive
is one of the most important tools. If you use it to your
advantage, it's rewarding. If you practice replacing negative
thoughts with positive ones, it can become a healthy habit,
while dwelling on the negative only invites more of the
same.

I like to be with people who are positive thinkers, and with those special people who lift my spirits up. It feels good to be around them. It rubs off on me. When I meet someone who glows with a sense of well being, I am drawn to that person. I want to find out more about what makes them tick.

On the other hand, when I am with someone who is inclined to be negative, and doesn't seem to want to change their way of thinking, I find that I quickly move away from that person's presence. I feel like time is too valuable to waste on negative thinking. Spending too much time in the company of someone whose energy leans toward the negative, can also rub off on you.

The challenge is to be able to think positively even when life has been unfair to you. Life very often doesn't seem fair. When it knocks you down, the trick is not to allow it to keep you down. If you persevere, you'll be the one who benefits from doing so.

Walt's mom was a perfect example of that kind of perseverance. She was a woman who still possessed, in her 80's, a child-like sense of wonder. When you were in her company, that sense of wonder became contagious. This woman who had lost both her husband and her son in the same year, still carried with her at all times, an absolute delight in the beauty and wonder of life.

I remember the day she had just had new dentures put in her mouth. Her mouth kept bleeding, and she was in a lot of pain, but I never heard a complaint out of her. She calmly kept replacing the gauze packs in her mouth with new ones. I came into the kitchen to check on her and found her so excited that she could hardly contain herself.

She said, "You won't believe what just happened. Two goldfinches came to the birdfeeder! Isn't that wonderful?"

It was so typical of her to find something not only to be happy about, but to delight in, even while dealing with pain. She had an abiding sense of appreciation of everything and everyone around her. She was always genuinely interested in what you had to say and in what was going on. She remained that way until she died at 91 years old. It was fun just being in her company.

My admiration ran deep for that wonderful woman whose birthday was one day before mine, thirty years prior. We had the very same interests: family, home, cooking, gardening, knitting and crocheting. When she'd come to visit, she'd tell me that she was going to bring her 'fancy work' so that we could sit and talk and keep our hands busy while doing so. Sometimes we'd sit by the lake and crochet and never say a word, but the space we shared while doing so was always filled with love.

SNOW FALLING

Fields of snow walk on water,
leading to some future destination.
I feel a heart bursting joy inside, anticipating.
Peace and love and all that is
surround me as your arms do
and mine encircle your neck,
while my head rests on your shoulder.

Layers of softly falling snow
cloak the air as my eyes take it in,
and I feel a quietness within me--
the comfort of just being with you.
Safe within your arms,

I lay down every burden I have ever known
and sense a deep abiding oneness with you.

The stillness of a winter day's beauty
inscribes upon our hearts
this peace that is ours to hold and absorb.
It is at once all encompassing.
Whirling wisps of snow fall and melt
upon the glowing warmth of our two hearts
as we take each other in....

Chapter 28

"I love you in order to begin to love you,
to start infinity again and to never stop loving you."
Pablo Neruda

A few years after Walt died, I fell hopelessly, madly, and completely in love-- for a second time-- with a man I had loved in my past. The first time we fell in love with each other was in high school when we were young. We were so young that many might have said we had no idea what love was all about. Although Nat King Cole sang at that time, "They tried to tell us we're too young, too young to really be in love," we really were in love.

I'd never expected to feel that kind of love again. When you are covered in that kind of love, people can't help but notice it in your face and in your countenance. It was the kind of love that made me feel like I was capable of doing anything, that nothing was impossible to me. I felt like I wanted to be the best person I could be so that he would be proud of me.

After we parted again, the ensuing grief rivaled any former grief I'd ever experienced. It was deeper and more heart-wrenching than anything that had gone before. Although our time together was brief in the course of a lifetime, my love for him was so powerful that it couldn't be assuaged without a monumental effort on my part.

He had come out of my past and into the present when my heart was still sad over Walt's death. He brought me more joy than I'd ever known. I was so happy that I often felt like I was walking on air. When I woke up in the morning I'd smile when I remembered he was in my life, and then I'd throw my arms up in the air and jump for joy! I was sure he had come to save me, but that was not the case. He had come to teach me more about life.

One beautiful summer day I'd gone to my mailbox and found, to my complete surprise, a note from him. He had written to tell me that a mutual friend of ours had died. I hadn't heard from him or the friend that had died, in years. Although I didn't know exactly how many years had passed since I'd seen him last, he did. He took my sister and me to lunch, and we talked, laughed, and looked at old photos I'd saved of us from long ago. The connection I felt to our past was uncanny.

He came into my life with the promise of something new and exciting, while at the same time appearing as someone familiar and cherished. We'd been so close, one long ago summer when we were young. We had parted when he went off to college. When he came back into my life I realized that I'd been looking for him in everyone I'd ever met. I think that your first love becomes a marker for how you judge other loves that follow. When it happens the first time there is nothing else to compare with. Your first love, if it was a good one, becomes something you judge subsequent ones by even when you aren't aware of it.

When I realized that was what I'd been doing all my life, I could hardly believe that he'd come and found me again. We discovered that our paths had come close to crossing a few times but it had never happened. It hadn't been the right time, I guess. This time I'd written a special request in my journal, just two weeks before his note. I prayed for someone to come that I could love. The synchronicity of events that followed was unbelievable!

I wasn't ready for such a magnificent experience to come and go so quickly, though. Sadly, he had to leave. He was already committed. When he wrote me the note he had only wanted to see how I was doing. He hadn't known beforehand that I was a widow.

He was a man of immense integrity, a very real person, totally in charge of things yet very much at ease with himself. Those were just a few of the attributes I loved about him. Most importantly, because he was a man who truly loved his family, I couldn't fault him for honoring his commitments.

I look back and try to discern how it could have gone differently. I thought that maybe I had done something wrong, yet I knew inside it wasn't about me at all. It was about the make-up of that remarkable man who came and showed me how wonderful it felt to be cherished. I will never again be the same woman I was before he came back into my life, and even though I was sad for a very long time, I wouldn't have given up the experience for the world.

We stayed in contact for a while even though I didn't see him any more. I sent him e-mails now and then, something that couldn't have happened years ago. I loved that he was still my friend, but I hated that he was only my friend. He was someone who knew me well and always understood how I felt. Because of that I had come to rely on his being there as a cushion, to catch me whenever I fell down.

In my heart I was always hoping something would change. Hope is a belief of such magnitude that it survives in places where nothing else can. It is often hidden in a corner of our heart even when we don't acknowledge it. If he wrote to me, that hope surfaced whenever I tried to read between the lines. Consequently, I would often feel sad and down in the dumps when I didn't hear from him at all. The written contact with him had the ability to fill my sails in its breeze or leave them hanging limp with the absence of it. It began to govern my daily moods.

One night I had a dream that woke me suddenly. In the dream there loomed before me, a huge iron gate about ten feet tall. Flowers were growing on the sides, but as I viewed the gate they disappeared and only the massiveness and strength of the gate remained. There was a quick 'knowing' inside me about the meaning of the closed gate. The time for holding on was over. The gate was closed and I couldn't go inside. I stopped writing to him. It wasn't just about my letting go, but about accepting that he was already gone.

When the memory of that beautiful time in my life comes in, I let it linger now and then. It no longer breeds despair. It goes quietly away when I bid it to. I don't keep company with its grief any longer. My days are no longer governed by words I might receive on a screen, and my thoughts aren't sent off to a person who lives a life that doesn't include me.

Sometimes I can still feel his pride in me and his encouragement in my endeavors. He lingers around the fringes of my being. That has to be enough. I am happy that he is alive and well, living in this world, and that I have not lost him irretrievably to death.

☙

IF I LOVE YOU

If I love you more than you can bear, and let loose
my unbridled heart to soar up into the heavens
with an all encompassing love for you, and it is hard
for you to accept, I hope that you will pardon me.

If I keep you deep inside of me where no person,
place, or thing can ever extricate you from me,
and know that the very thought of you is coupled with
my every breath, I beg you to indulge me.

If I cannot hide or keep my love from surfacing
in every word I send to you, and know that doing so
leaves rifts upon your heart, I ask for you to forgive me.

If I laugh or cry and cause you to do so
along with me because we are one, and I let you know
through time and space that it is so, please don't harden
your heart to me and make my soul cry out in anguish.

If I love you to what seems like distraction,
accept that it may very well be true.
Believe that it is as natural to me as smiling,
as fundamental as opening my eyes in the morning,
and as necessary to me as believing
that God is somewhere watching over us.

For you see, I never came to be without the need
to love you my whole life through.
You are my shelter and my fortress, my strength
and my weakness, my beginning and my ending.
I do not exist alone.

As my feet make tracks in the brown earth,
I do not have life in my steps without you
co-existing inside of me.
When I lay down in the sweet-smelling green grass,
I do not even feel its softness, unless I have you
embedded in my skin to experience it with me.

I do not sense the velvet night as it covers me,
no matter how beautiful it might be,
unless I sense the splendor of your memorized form
covering me as well.

I do not choose it to be this way, unless
somewhere unknown to me, I did, but instead it seems
that it chose me, and my delight is boundless because it is
so.
There has never been a time remembered inside of me,
where I existed without you, my Beloved.

You are in the blood that courses through my body.
You are the warmth I feel beside me
and all around me when I sleep at night.

Because I love you so, and because you are such a part of
me,
I accept life as it unfolds without complaint.
I simply am who I am, and I know that I am to love you
with all that I have and all that I am, my whole life
through.
That is a truth I know.

Chapter 29

"Dedicate yourself to the good you
deserve and desire for yourself. Give
yourself peace of mind. You deserve
to be happy. You deserve delight."
Mark Victor Hansen

Spring had arrived, or so it seemed to me. When that long-awaited warmth engulfed me as I opened the door to step outside, I knew it was finally here. The winter had retreated at last. It didn't matter that the weather man had said that by the end of the week we could have snow again. In spite of that possibility, we all knew that since it was the middle of April, spring wouldn't be leaving.

When I sat down by the water in the sun that morning, I knew the day was definitely a harbinger of things to come. Luckily, my little deck is partially surrounded by a cinder block wall that protects me from the wind, even in the colder days. If the sun is out, I can sit there with my face turned toward its warmth, my eyes closed, and my heart full of that sense of timelessness that always comes to me by the water.

This spring day would be one of the last days where the lake belonged just to me and the wildlife. I heard the geese honking at each other, I watched the grebes bobbing around on the small, choppy waves, and I knew that soon it would all be different. Saturday was Opening Day for fishing season.

Saturday, at 5:30 in the morning, the fishermen would all be lined up at the state boat launch, ready to embark on a morning of fishing for the first time this spring. Most of them would catch their quota swiftly, as the lake had just been stocked, and then they would be on their way to, maybe, another fishing spot. With all the activity arriving on the lake, it would no longer feel like it belonged to me alone.

I always enjoy calling it "my lake". Sometimes I wonder why more people don't come and enjoy its peace. I sat there that day, listening to the quiet, sensing only the sounds of the birds in the background, knowing it would all be different soon. The appearance of the lake changes with every season.

As I looked out over the lake that Walt had loved so much, I wondered what my life would be like today if he hadn't died. He came so close to being everything my heart desired. Life with Walt was good and fun, and even okay when I had to take care of him in the end. The memories of those last few months--when taking care of him was a difficult task--didn't come back to haunt me as much any more, now that enough time had passed.

What does haunt me is the fact that I sit here alone, looking out over the lake. It's not that I don't love my times alone, especially in this beautiful place, it's the fact that no one is sitting beside me, holding my hand and enjoying the idyllic view with me. I yearn for that. I once told Walt that I would have married him even without the bonus of this lake, but that I was glad it came with him. I am forever grateful that marrying him brought me to such a beautiful spot.

On a spring evening, as the sky begins to darken and the full moon comes up over the lake, I sit by the water, lost in thought. The moon seems to demand that someone be with me to gaze at it, to put their arm around me and squeeze my shoulder as we stand side by side, viewing it.

Being alone is only good when it's by choice. Being alone when you wish you were with someone is rarely out of choice. At times when I have felt the loneliest, I realize that some of the circumstances of my life simply haven't afforded me the choice. I stand wistfully by the lake, the moonlight soft around me, cloaked in nostalgia.

SOMEBODY'S SOMEONE

I would like to be somebody's someone.
I would like to love again and be loved back.
I would like to meet somebody's eyes
as they connect with mine across a room.

I would like to be somebody's partner.
I would like to find a love to be my own.
I would like to feel a touch and know
such joy that I cannot believe it's true.

I would like to be somebody's soulmate.
I would like to know a love that fills my heart.
I would like to be somebody's dream
and know that they'd be glad to be mine, too.

I would like to be somebody's someone.
I would like to walk with them beside the sea.
I would like to rest with arms so safe
that I would always know that I was home.

Chapter 30

"The language of friendship is
not words but meanings."
Henry David Thoreau

A few years ago, a friend of mine died of a heart attack
at 49 years of age. I hadn't seen her in a while as time and
changes in our lifestyles had separated us over the years.
Whenever we ran into each other or talked on the phone,
we would promise to get together soon. We always meant
to. It wasn't because we didn't care, and it wasn't because
we didn't want it to happen, it was just that we didn't act
on it. We only thought about it. There is nothing sadder
than the feeling that comes over you when you hear that a
friend has died, and you know you've missed your chance
to see them again. You've lost out because you were remiss
in keeping up with the friendship.

We are so busy in our lives with so many things to do
and so many tasks requiring our attention. There are many
people who, although they are merely acquaintances, still
demand some of our time. It's no wonder there isn't any
time left to spend with our friends. The time is there if
we arrange our priorities in the right order. The people
that really matter should take precedence over those who
don't. We are only allowed so much time on this earth. It's
a shame to spend precious time with those around us who
might not even cry at our funeral, and neglect those who
would.

I cried at my friend's funeral. I cried in church when I heard that she had died. I cried for myself, and I cried for my loss. She had once sat next to me in that very church when I brought her there. She hadn't been there for a long time, and I hadn't called to invite her to join me, either. When I sat in church and heard about her death, I remembered the words of a poem I'd memorized in high school. The words seemed so very appropriate.

AROUND THE CORNER

Around the corner I have a friend
in this great city that has no end.
Yet days go by, and weeks rush on,
and before I know it a year is gone,
And I never see my old friend's face,
for life is a swift and terrible race.
He knows I like him just as well as in the days
when I rang his bell and he rang mine.
We were younger then,
but now we are busy, tired men:
Tired with playing a foolish game,
tired with trying to make a name.
"Tomorrow," I say," I will call on Jim,
just to show that I'm thinking of him."
But tomorrow comes and tomorrow goes,
and the distance between us grows and grows.
Around the corner!.. yet miles away...
"Here's a telegram, sir..."
"Jim died today."
And that's what we get, and deserve in the end:

around the corner,
a vanished friend.

Charles Hanson Towne

My friend had gone to Florida on a week's vacation. She had called her family to tell them what glorious weather they were having there. It was sunny and warm, and she was about to go out and enjoy the day. She never lived to see another one.

When her family said good-bye to her as she left for her vacation, they had no idea that they would never have the chance to say hello to her again. That kind of pain must have been excruciatingly painful. It was the kind of grief I saw in the eyes of her husband and her children at her funeral service.

There is nothing quite as hard to bear as the shock of unexpected death. There is no way to be prepared for it. After 9/11, that was the kind of shock so many people experienced, over the loss of their loved ones. Not disregarding the fact that the horrific event shocked the whole world, the personal anguish was monumental. So many people had innocently said, "Good-bye" to loved ones that morning, never dreaming they would never get to say, "Hello", again.

Living today, as if there might not be a tomorrow, is a good way to remember to make the most out of what we have right now, right here; but it's easily forgotten in our busy lives. We need to treat each day as a precious gift. We should never put off a kindness to anyone. We should treat life respectfully, with the knowledge that it could be taken away in an instant. We are often poignantly reminded, as I was, when my friend died.

When time begins to separate us from the event, we are often apt to revert back to taking life for granted and thinking somehow that we will live forever. Death exists as something so far down the road that we pay it no mind. We pay it no mind, until it touches us once again. Despite reminder upon reminder, we still don't seem to be able to keep on top of living life to the fullest, every day.

After my friend's death, I'd felt the need to e-mail some of my other friends, and renew our connections, especially those from my past. I made a promise to try to prevent another missed opportunity like that of my lost friend.

A college reunion was coming up, and it was a perfect time to get together with the friends from my college days. There had been eight of us who were good friends and remained so throughout the years. We'd lost one of the eight to Multiple Sclerosis, and then there were seven of us. After she was diagnosed with M.S., we tried to get together as often as we could, knowing there could come a day when we might lose her.

The friend who was taking charge of making sure we all went to the reunion had been battling cancer for a long time, and we were well aware of the fragile nature of her life also. Two weeks before the reunion, as if to prove that we should always be mindful, came the heart-breaking news that she had died. Six of us remained.

I went to her funeral with her roommate from college, one of the six. We spent eleven hours in the car together that day. The funeral service was uplifting, though sad. The two of us decided that we wanted to celebrate her life by making sure we found time to celebrate our own while we were still alive. We have done just that, taking time out from our busy schedules, to get together when we can

We've changed over the years, but are still the same. Today we carry our water bottles and our cell phones and do our part to insure a good life on this planet for our grandchildren. We became friends because we gravitated toward each other and we have remained friends because we love each other.

Connecting with people we have been close to in the past, but have lost touch with over the years, can be such a rewarding experience. We don't have to explain to them who we are, because they know us already. The bond established early on, is more secure than any other. Life gets so busy and time seems so scarce. We try to spread ourselves too thin sometimes, but it's always worth taking time out of our busy schedules to spend time with old friends.

WHO WOULD HAVE THOUGHT

If you always thought that America was
invulnerable to attack, and that
the price of freedom was already paid,
then you must think again.

If you thought that deeds of hate and fear
only happened somewhere else,
and you didn't need to care or concern yourself,
then you must think again.

If you thought that structures standing tall,
proclaiming who we are,
were indestructible and couldn't be demolished,
now you must think again.

If you never gave much thought
to the part you play in living in
America, or about your responsibility
to your fellow man,
then you must think again.

If you thought that good-byes to loved ones
meant you'd say hello again
and never had to doubt that they'd be safe 'til then,
then sadly, think again.

If you thought that "purple mountain's majesty
and amber waves of grain"
were only words to sing, and never caught their meaning,
then think on it again.

If red, white, and blue and flags unfurled
never caused your heart to swell
with pride for what it means to be an American,
today you know the truth.

If you took it for granted that
"life, liberty and the pursuit of happiness"
were ours to claim because we live in America,
you must protect that right.

Chapter 31

"I expect to pass through this world but once.
Any good therefore that I can do, or any kindness
I can show to any fellow-creature, let me do it now.
Let me not defer or neglect it, for I shall not pass this
way again."
Stephen Grellet

To talk, to converse, to open the door so the story can come through; that's what interests us and unites us. Although most people don't strike up a conversation about death, dying, and loss upon meeting someone new, it doesn't necessarily mean they're not interested in talking about it. People are interested in the stories others have to tell, and many have stories of their own to share about such happenings.

A while ago I met someone and the conversation turned to the amazing fortitude and strength of so many women who have encountered tragedy and strife in their lives. I launched into a dissertation about a good friend who had lost her 18-year-old daughter, when the car she was driving home one rainy, fall evening, slid off the road and hit a tree. My heart fills with admiration for this friend, not only because of her inner strength in the face of such terrible grief, but for her ever cheerful countenance which has survived her monumental loss.

After her daughter's death, she established a scholarship in her name. To this day, she continues to bring up all the endearing qualities about her in conversation, and always makes people feel at ease when her daughter's name is brought up. I consider her a living, breathing example of a 'lover of life' in spite of the tragedy it handed her.

My new acquaintance responded with an accounting of her nephew's accidental death in Africa when he was just a young man. After his death, because he had had such a rapport with the elephants, his family created a foundation in his name for research regarding the elephants. Gestures such as these that benefit others after a loved one has died help alleviate the pain, especially when the death has been a tragedy.

Often there's the big question of 'why' when a death has been untimely. Although the answer may elude us, in retrospect we sometimes catch a glimpse of something worthwhile and fulfilling coming out of the sorrow. So much good has been done because of people's need to honor the lives and memories of loved ones who have died.

I have a friend who's a lawyer. She told me that when she became a lawyer, she thought she was going to save the world. She found out very quickly that wasn't going to be the case. But, she did do something else in her own little corner of the world that, in the long run, probably meant much more than saving the whole world. A family member had been involved in physical abuse and because of that, my friend had been instrumental in creating a place in her area where battered women could go and be safe. Because of her love and concern, she used a terrible situation to establish something of great value to others.

When she and I talked about this, we both agreed that the extent of the good we do doesn't have to be widespread, it only has to serve someone else. What happens afterward, as a result of something good being done for mankind, is often a foundation for the ripple effect. A single good deed could end up spreading world-wide for all we know. It has only to be passed on.

I send $30 a month to an Episcopal diocese in South Africa, a place where it is not unusual for children to lose both parents to AIDS. I have been doing so ever since I met the bishop and his wife when they came to my church to speak. The bishop spoke of people who walked for many, many, miles to his church, to receive money to help them out. Each person received what amounted to less than a dollar! I was appalled by the meager amount and struck by the fact that I probably wasted at least a dollar a day!

In Western Tanganyika, there are countless children who have been orphaned because of this dreadful disease. Not only did our church pledge to help with the education of these children, but I personally decided to give a dollar a day for the bishop to use in any way he saw fit, possibly to help a widow whose husband had died of AIDS.

At the end of my first year of doing this, the bishop wrote me the following letter which brought me to tears:

Dear Cindy;
In January I gave a parishioner $ 300 being 10 months collection of your gifts.
She is a daughter of one of my retired priests. She has gone through hell in life due to being married to an abusive husband. She left her husband last year and stayed for a while with her sister who was a school teacher. Unfortunately her sister died of AIDS in November last year and left her helpless.
So when the church began to pray for her and to seek ways on how to help, and when she came to my office to tell her sad story, I was so moved that I decided to

help her. She has now set-up a small business which is doing very well. She said if her business gets better she would also like to contribute and help another lady or AIDS widow because she is so grateful to find her life back again. She has three small lovely kids and in three months only she is now able to feed and cloth her kids. She has even gone to court to seek divorce so that she can part completely with this abusive husband. Before your help she could not trust in herself and was afraid to go to court. Your help has made such a big difference in her life and she has strong confidence in herself.

So Cindy thank you for saving her life. I wish she spoke English because she would have written to you. However I have asked her to send you photos of herself and her kids.

It humbled me when I realized that my seemingly small contribution, promoted in part by my experience with Walt dying of AIDS, had made such a profound difference in someone else's life.

WITH YOU

I let you go a thousand times
yet call you back for more.
I send away my heart with you
and wonder where it's stored.

I find you in a hundred songs
and wonder where you've gone.

I sing the words as if to you
but you are not along.

I feel you in each breath I take
and in each thing I do
I walk alone, but not apart
from what I have with you.

I pay my debt to loneliness
and conjure up its fee.
I trod the pathways of my heart
and there you are with me.....

Chapter 32

"I want to know if you can sit with pain,
mine or your own, without moving to
hide it or fade it, or fix it."
Oriah Mountain Dreamer, <u>The Invitation</u>

One day, just before Christmas, I met up with the woman who had called me and asked for help after her husband died--the woman who had the child to care for. It was Christmastime and she had just crossed my mind when I saw her name in my Christmas card list. Every year since her husband had died I'd sent a Christmas card to her and her daughter.

It was just two weeks before Christmas, and my mind had been busy sorting through the many tasks I had set for myself to do. My car interrupted by making a strange noise and I decided it would be a good idea to stop and have it checked at my garage. A woman passed by me while I was standing in the office, and a name came to mind. I realized it was her daughter's name, but I couldn't remember hers. I wanted to say hello, after not seeing her for four years, so I asked my mechanic her name.

I walked over to where she was standing, picking up a tire that she had left to be repaired. I greeted her, gave her a hug, and asked how she was. She answered in a low-key voice, saying she was okay. Something seemed wrong.

So I asked, cheerily, how her daughter was, knowing she had been the bright spot in her life after her husband's death, five years prior. "She died", she said to me, "just this past September". My astonishment was so great that I thought I must have asked about the wrong person. I said, "How old was she?" She replied, "Nineteen", and I knew that I had the right girl.

She told me that her daughter had been in the hospital and had picked up an infection. Two days after she had come home, she had died in her sleep. My mouth dropped open in disbelief, and I could find no appropriate words to say. Any words of consolation seemed futile. I knew exactly what her tortured look said. It told me she was just passing through life at the moment, numb inside and not connecting to anything around her.

What do you say to a young woman who has lost her husband and her daughter in the space of five years? How do you even begin to assimilate the enormous impact of such a tragedy? How does a parent live with the loss of a child? Why would God give one person so much to bear? I thought instantly of my mother-in-law, who had lost her husband, and her son, in the space of six months. I thought of my mom, who had lost her son in his early thirties. I realized it didn't matter what the age, when a child dies before a parent, the first question that comes to mind is, "Why not me instead?"

I stood and I talked with her about that and tried to find some comforting words to say to her. All I could do was remind her about the one thing she had already learned; that she would get through it, not necessarily over it, but through it. She was already familiar with that process of dragging herself out of bed every day, from that time when she had lost her husband.

I hugged her once more before we parted and told her to call me and come down and visit me, and sit with me by my lake, at some point. She agreed to do that sometime.

I got in my car and drove away, expecting to carry on with my many tasks. But they had suddenly become very unimportant. I drove around in a daze, tears sliding down my cheeks, wondering how I would ever handle such a thing as losing one of my children. We take our children's health and safety for granted, sometimes, especially when they are grown up and out of our house. I've never been a worrier, so I never went to a negative place where I feared for their safety. I'd always trusted that God would keep watching over them, just as I believed He had while they were growing up.

I couldn't shake the empathy I felt over this woman's grief. The holidays, coming up soon, would be sad for her. I remembered the Christmas after David had died, when I was so lucky to have had Mark and Uschi living with me, and the arrival of their new baby to look forward to. Then I remembered the Christmas after Walt had died, and I came in touch once again, with the emptiness of a joyous season, spent in sadness.

I thought about each of my five children, and how precious their lives were to me. I just sat in a parking lot and shook my head. Could I ever handle that kind of grief? I said a fervent prayer that I would never have to. I was sure that no matter what I had been through in the past, I would never be able to handle that kind of grief.

Maybe it was meant to be about perspective, this happening that socked me in the stomach that day, amidst my Christmas shopping and planning. The obvious grief and terrible sorrow of this woman made any problem I might have had seem immaterial.

The focus of my day changed. It didn't seem important any more to run around from store to store, making purchases for the upcoming holiday. It was as if I had sifted through the debris of activity I'd planned and thrown out all the unimportant things. I was left with a feeling of humbleness that comes when we are reminded of how fleeting life can be. It was as if life had come to a halt, and I had stopped to look around to see what really mattered. I stopped at a nursing home to visit an old friend and was rewarded by the delighted look on his face when I appeared. We shared a warm and gratifying visit.

The next day after I'd experienced this woman's grief first hand, I renewed my commitment to living life to the fullest. I felt a calm peaceful feeling about my life and my blessings. I thanked God again for watching over my children as they went along with their lives.

That evening my middle son, Scott, called to tell me he'd had an accident with his big truck on a busy highway. He was shaken up but fine. One of the tires had come off his truck while he was driving. He was carrying a load of concrete slabs and the state trooper kept saying it was a miracle his truck hadn't rolled over, and that he hadn't been killed. He was also amazed that no one else on the highway had been involved. I knew after talking to him about his close call, that he was looking at his life differently that evening.

For a minute I thought of how it would have been if I were standing in my family room, getting ready to put up my Christmas tree and someone had to call me and inform me that my son had had a fatal accident. I shuddered as I remembered that sad woman once more, the one who had no answers for her daughter's death.

REMEMBERING YOU

Shivers of memory,
Bounty of bliss,
Agates of heart fire,
Felt from your kiss.

Movements so gentle,
Stored from each year,
Bind us together...
Place with no fear.

Ever so perfectly
Pieces become
Part of each other...
Meant to be one.

Love is the present
Offered each time
That you embrace me...
Yours becomes mine.

Safe through forever,
Born on this day,
Hearts so committed
Constant will stay.

Chapter 33

"We never know the love of our
parents for us till we become parents."
Henry Ward Beecher

When my dad died a few years ago, we took my mom's ashes with us to his memorial service. She traveled there in a little black box on my niece's lap. My niece announced that she had 'Nanie' with her as we set out in our caravan of cars. My mom had died eight months before my dad, but we had never gotten around to putting her ashes in the ground. It was her wish to be buried with her parents, so we had decided it would be appropriate to put her ashes in the cemetery where they were buried after the service and burial of my dad's ashes.

Dad and Mom had been divorced from each other for many years and had each remarried. Both of their respective spouses had died. My dad lived alone and my mom was in a nursing home. My sister and I often picked them both up to go out to dinner, or for a family gathering. In their old age, they were sweet to each other, having had many years in common, plus a mellowing as they grew older. The four of us had fun spending time together, once again.

My mom was an energetic woman who hated to be left out of anything that went on, even if it wasn't meant to include her. She just loved to be in the middle of things. Even when her aging body said, "No", her lively mind still thought it was possible. It was fitting, that the black box with her ashes should accompany us to my dad's service. She would have loved it.

It was a day of closure. After attending the graveside service for my dad, and leaving his ashes with his beloved second wife, we trooped off to another cemetery and set my mom to rest next to her mother and father. Under the shade of a row of lovely trees, the small group of people joining my sister and I included some of our children and aunts. We stood in a circle and held hands. I read the words from the Bible, "To everything there is a season", and we sent her on her way.

My grieving was minimal for these two people who I loved, and who were responsible in so many ways for the person I am today. Their journey had gotten tedious over the last few years, especially my mom's. She died just before she turned 80. My dad died at 86. I did miss talking with Dad as I wistfully remembered the days before his second marriage, when I would go to him with my cares and concerns. He would listen quietly while I talked, just as he'd done in the days when I was growing up.

I actually didn't expect to miss my mom the way I did, as she could be exasperating at times. During the last few years of her life, my sister and I had spent many an hour visiting her in the nursing home. Fran would fix Mom up, making sure she was comfortable. I would sit in a chair, peacefully knitting. We'd often bring fancy cups, coffee in a thermos and cream, for a special get-together outside, if the weather permitted. We'd wheel Mom out in her wheelchair and sit in the sun laughing, talking, and enjoying our coffee together--something we'd done for years. When she died, she left behind a huge block of time in our lives--a vacancy that made her death more apparent to us. We had both given her so much of our time during the months preceding her death that the void was like a chasm.

Although I miss both my mom and dad I cannot despair that they have left this earthly place. I remember instead who they were and what they did for me, just by being my parents. I don't feel that any unresolved issues were left behind for me to deal with on my own. I'd long since forgiven anything there was to forgive. My mom wasn't very deep and most of her thoughts were spoken out loud!

I used to think that my mom never really let me know that she loved me, never praised me enough, never really knew who I was. I think she might have been afraid of spoiling me. It was an aspect of child raising that was typical of her generation. In my teenage years, when I was especially vulnerable to criticism, she told me that I shouldn't smile too much because my teeth were too big. What an impression my mother left on my tight lipped face. For years, I was self-conscious about smiling, especially when I met someone new. Heaven forbid that I should make a first impression that said only "TEETH!"

I wondered why my mother had been so adamant about this. Was she afraid of someone else making a joke about my teeth? Feeling a little like the ugly duckling, I asked my dad if he thought that I was beautiful. His reply fell short of the mark I wanted. He said, "You're cute, Cindy, but you'll never be beautiful." From that point on I yearned for someone to think I was beautiful. Throughout my life, if anyone ever said so, I was thrilled.

After my mom's death, I could see that I had been wrong about how I interpreted many of her interactions with me. I wish that I had known her heart better, but that was not the way our relationship was. With her death my perspective changed, and I saw much that I had never allowed myself to see while she was alive. Best of all, I was keenly aware that my mother had loved me.

When my father died, I sat in church during his memorial service and thought about how much he had meant to me. He had always been there for me and I had always known it. With his passing, all of that flooded back over me. I knew once again, something I had always known: that he was very much responsible for the woman I had become, by the way he had acted and treated me.

What my father didn't know was that I would always look for a certain type of love, because of how he loved me. His love for me was totally unconditional. He never judged me, which was the most important aspect of our relationship. He was one of a kind, a rarity among men, the kind of man who loved me from his heart, admired me for who I was and cherished me until the day he died.

My dad was a carpenter, a cabinet maker, a pattern maker and a master craftsman. When he was 18, he'd designed and built a small sail boat. In his 50's he decided he wanted to build a 32-foot boat, and perhaps sail it around the world--a dream he never realized.

He bought a fiberglass hull and built that sailboat up on a scaffold in the front yard of my parents' home one winter. Heavy plastic covered the structure to keep out the cold. I loved to go over to the house, climb up the ladder and sit with my cup of coffee or a drink, warm inside the enclosure, talking to my dad while he worked on his boat. Those times are some of my fondest memories. I was going through my divorce at that time and I valued his company and his listening ear. I realized that he had spent a good part of his life listening to me!

I silently thanked him as I sat there in the church. I thanked him for his part in helping me to be a better person. I thanked him for always being there when I needed someone to talk to. He'd had the ability to whittle monumental problems down to their proper size. He had always known how to put them into their proper prospective. Having such good memories to call on, and being able to smile about him, helped me to combat the sadness of losing him.

In the long run, it's all about love: my parents loving me, my spouse loving me, my children loving me, and my friends. It's about me loving them in return. Whoever we are, we all have the need to be loved and to love back. Today, when I remember my parents, I love them still, and I am more aware than ever of how much they loved me.

YOUR CIRCLE

I know that the circle which surrounds who you are
always surrounds me, too.
I travel its circumference and notice
my lengthening shadow as the sun begins to set.
I wonder if I am my shadow filled with gray space,
the sun at my back seeping through.

Your smile draws me into your circle and I hesitate,
not knowing if I should step inside.
Somehow I manage to stay outside the circle of you
and not be drawn into that place
where sweet green grass invites me in
but dusty earth reminds me it is bittersweet.

I return to the kingdom of reason
for it is powered by gravity and keeps me on my path.
It is only when I feel another's pain
that mine is capable of escaping, making me bleed.
Then I am reminded that loving endures and
because of that makes the price worthwhile.

Chapter 34

"Let us risk remembering that we never stop
silently loving those we once loved out loud."
Oriah Mountain Dreamer, The Dance

One morning, after months of a long winter-like
session of pain, I woke up and realized that something had
changed. I felt a new, yet remembered emotion, emerging.
I felt a sense of happiness! That day, I no longer lay in bed
wondering about whether to get up or not. I didn't have
to talk myself into the prospect of a happy day. It was just
there!

It was there in front of me as I swung my legs over the
side of the bed, stood up, stretched, and cautiously tested
the way I felt. I was concerned for a moment that I had
only fooled myself into thinking all was well. And then, an
overwhelming sense of well-being enveloped me. Someone
new and interesting had entered my life and suddenly the
whole world looked brighter.

I remembered all the lonely days I'd wished for
something like this to happen. I also remembered that for
so long I didn't want anyone new to come into my life, so
deep was my pain. But then, with time, I had allowed for
the possibility that someone new just might be the key for
finding happiness again. Disloyalty to a memory had often
gotten in the way of my positive thinking. Living in a past
that held so much happiness sometimes took precedent
over venturing out into the unknown to find someone
new.

There is no disloyalty in loving again. The experience of loving again can transcend death and loss. That we were meant to love and be loved is an undeniable truth. The ending of one love and the promise of another don't detract from each other. On the contrary, the more we love, the wider our capacity to love expands, and the wider our scope of awareness becomes.

This is the way it is with life. We were meant to love. We were fashioned that way. The grief over losing someone we loved can often cause us to be wary of loving again, lest we get hurt, but the infinite power within our hearts to love, like the capacity of the brain to store knowledge, is limitless. Most times we only scratch the surface. Yet, something deep inside of us still urges us to spend it lavishly and as often as possible.

In spite of the number of times that this type of awareness has become apparent to me, I am still always amazed. I am actually in awe of how capable the heart is at repairing itself, by opening up to the possibility of happiness and love again. I've arrived at a place where I'm willing to let the past go, allowing the beautiful parts of it to remain in my memory while not obscuring my view of the future. I can live right here and now, in this moment, making room for more incredible things to happen in my life.

❧

SEARCHING

I'd been waiting for you to arrive,
loving you long before you came.
Sometimes my heart felt stripped bare
without you to clothe it in love.

Sometimes I despaired of you coming at all;
yet all the time you were on your way,
coming ever so assuredly toward me,
maybe all of your life.

So desperately did I long for you,
that I didn't even notice when you arrived.
My soul tried to tell me so many times
but I ignored it as I widened my search.

Patiently you waited for me,
maybe even knowing that it was me
you had traveled so far to find.
Quietly you stayed until I knew.

Suddenly I was aware of a quickening inside
when I found you smiling at me,
and the realization that you had been there all along
swept over me as my heart opened wide.

Now a flooding of love and a knowing that it was you
I had been searching for all this time,
comes over me and engulfs me
every time I see your face and feel your hand touch my
hair.

Chapter 35

"I am discovering that I have exactly the right number of hours and minutes and seconds to accomplish and do everything that I need to do in my lifetime."
Claire Cloninger

If you haven't been a grandparent yet, you will not understand what it means to be one, or how it feels to hold a little one in your arms, that is a part of you--your child's child. When my sister became a grandmother for the very first time, she admitted to me that she had always considered me a bit foolish and overbearing with my many photos and constant chatter about my grandchildren. When it became her turn, she said to me, "I didn't know. I had no idea!" That was when her six-month-old grandson and his parents were visiting her for the first time and living at her house. She said that when she was out with him, she had the urge to tell everyone in the store that he was her grandson, as if they couldn't tell simply by observing her with him!

What she understood when it became her turn to be a grandparent, was the absolute thrill of being with your own grandchild. It's everything it's cracked up to be and more! The first time you hold that small body, hot as a little furnace, smelling of milk and making gurgling sounds, you're aware that you are holding a little life in your arms. Then you look upon the little face and form of one you cannot help but love with all your heart, a little person who is part of you-- and you know that this is what it's all about.

It might be a time to make amends without even knowing it, for all the little things you neglected to do with your own children. You might not have been able to give them the same kind of attention, because you were so busy raising them. Concerned about who they would become, you were involved in trying to make everything work out right.

What occurs is a softening of the heart--especially for men--because of the freedom to express the love you feel, without any inhibitions. By the time we become grandparents, most of us have become aware of how short life really is, and how fast the years fly by. If you've lost a loved one to death, it's even more apparent. We're also cognizant of all the precious moments that were lost, because of work and obligations. Having been robbed of time with our children, we're acutely aware that we can never recapture it again—and so we delight in giving that time back to our children's children.

Spending time with grandchildren gives you a chance to enjoy all the wonderful attributes children have to offer and find joy in being with them. Sometimes with the little ones, it's just a treat to sit and watch them. The best part is that you can say good-bye when it's time to go, and leave the responsibility of raising them to your own children. It isn't that you're not concerned; it's just that you know it's not your turn this time. That fact gives you the freedom to love them, unconditionally, and even spoil them a little!

When Walt died, I spent the next year vacationing and visiting my children who lived out of state. I'd come home for a few weeks; but when the sorrow I experienced in my familiar surroundings became too unbearable, I was off again to another place where I could forget about pain. Two months after Walt's death, I was vacationing in Florida when my oldest daughter, Michelle, called me to tell me that she and her husband were going to have a baby, their first, in September. My joy was immeasurable by any standard! Something wonderful was coming to fill in that huge gaping hole inside of me, and it would be the most blessed of gifts, a little child.

That day I began a diary, written to my then unborn grandchild, telling that child how much she was already loved by me. (I didn't know until later that she would be a girl.) Whenever I felt sad, I would write in my little book, a small notebook that my daughter had given me for my Florida trip. On the day my granddaughter was born, I wrote in it, recording my feelings toward her. That was a day where joy also knew no measure!

I had given birth to five children, but nothing compared with the experience of watching my granddaughter enter this world. When they put her in the incubator, she was wailing. I was the first one to ever talk to her. When I went over to her I said, "Don't cry, Sarah. You're going to love it here." She stopped crying. When I observed her beautiful little face, I could tell that she was listening to the sound of my voice. My heart swelled with such love for this precious child that I was struck with an awareness of a bond of love that she and I would always share.

I intend to give that little diary to my beloved Sarah, when she is a teenager. I've written in it whenever I've seen her, which is not nearly as much as I'd like to as she lives out of state. I've recorded how I've felt when I've been with her, and I've written down little anecdotes which, if unrecorded, might be lost in the passing of time. I want her to know when she grows up how dearly I've loved her ever since the day her mom told me she was to be born. Her small, sweet presence after she was born helped to alleviate the burden of grief I'd been feeling over the loss of Walt.

My 20-year-old grandson, Patrick, is also a delight to me. Over six feet tall, he bends down to hug me and says, "Hello, Grandmother, dear", whenever he sees me. His dad was in the army for over 20 years and I only got to see him once a year if I was lucky, because they were always stationed so far away. Toward the end of my son's army career, he ended up being stationed as a recruiter in the same town he had been recruited from, 15 minutes away from me! Don't let anyone ever tell you prayer doesn't work! After that, my grandson lived 45 minutes away from me while he was in high school, and I happily attended any event he was involved in.

Patrick graduated from high school a few years ago and went off to college. His dad turned 40 just before that. I remember how young his mom and dad seemed when he was born, but what I remember more is what a blessing it was to have them living in my home with that baby, after David's death.

When he was a senior in high school, I was complaining to my daughter, Laura, on our way up to Mark and Uschi's house for supper, about not having as many grandchildren as a friend whose 60th birthday party I had just attended. I said I understood now what had concerned my mother in her later years. It was the fact that she wanted to be able to see and know all her grandchildren and maybe some of her great-grandchildren, but was afraid she wouldn't live long enough to have that wish fulfilled.

As we sat down for coffee, my son remarked that he'd

heard I was kind of bent out of shape about not having any more grandchildren. (I just had two at the time.) Whatever my comment was, it was lost in the next breath. They informed me that when Patrick turned 18, they would be obliging me the next week by having a baby. When I laughed, my daughter-in-law said, "It's true. I will be wheeling a baby carriage to graduation." I don't think that I will ever forget how incredulous I was, as my mouth dropped open in disbelief. I reiterate that we have no idea of the amazing things that can happen in our lives, at any time!

That precious little boy, Josh, was born in February, right on schedule. When I held him on the first day of his life, I looked right into his eyes and made another amazing connection with another grandchild. Every time that I've seen him since has been filled with delight. To hear him exclaim, "Gramma!" when he first sees me, is probably one of my greatest joys.

My son, Scott, and his wife, Chrissy, presented me with my fourth grandchild last year. The year before, they had gotten married in the Napa Valley, in California, where 50 of us had gone to join them for the joyful occasion. A few months later, they announced that they would be having a baby in the summer. I think I was almost as excited as they were!

Little Grace Elisabeth is no exception when it comes to joy. Watching her grow is another one of the delights of my life! Although Scott and Chrissy moved out of state not too long after she was born, every time I see her is exciting for me. Watching her grow, along with the other grandchildren, stands out as one of life's most bountiful blessings.

LITTLE ONE

Little angel, lying there,
Bundled up with utmost care,
Bright eyes looking out at me,
Quizzically, "Where can I be?"

Tiny fingers, tiny toes,
Smelling fragrant, like a rose.
I will keep you safe, my Love.
God will watch you from above.

All the love within unfolds,
Fills my heart, as now I hold,
Close to me, your precious form,
Little baby, soft and warm.

I will watch you as you grow,
Sharing all the things I know.
Sweetheart, you remind me of,
That little child, your Gramma loved.

Chapter 36

"If I had my life to live over I would
start barefoot earlier in the spring and stay
that way later in the fall...I would ride more
merry-go-rounds. I would pick more daisies."
Nadine Stair

I arrive at my favorite place. The ocean and the sandbars stretch out in front of me, beckoning me to come and walk. It's fall. I've come full circle and passed the summer by again. "Where did all the people go?" I wonder. It's as if on Labor Day they all pivoted and walked away, never to return until Memorial Day, at the beginning of summer the next year.

It isn't cold. It's windy but very sunny, and I am dressed for the weather in layers and cut-off pants with my bare feet still longing to sink themselves into the wet sand. The sandbars sprawl out, reaching from beach to beach, fringed with seagulls on the outer edges. They are lined up in rows, saluting the radiating sun.

I march along, exercising my physical body; when in truth, I come here to exercise my soul. It flies free as I walk, just like the gulls who, fluffed up, facing the sinking afternoon sun, take off in unison as I approach.

No one is there walking except me. So much open space with a sky adorned with twists of cotton candy clouds, here and there. "Where is everybody?" I say aloud to the wind as it blows strands of my hair across my face. It's early fall, and the water between the sandbars, that feels like bath water in the summer time, is still only slightly cool on my feet. I shuffle through it.

This is a place of memory for me. For over 50 years I have come here. I think my soul must reside here most of the time. The ripples of the sandbars left by the receding waters of the tide, remind me of the ripples of sorrow and pain left on my heart from the tides of life. Like the sandbars, I await the turn of the tide. Then my heart becomes smoothed over, all hurt gone, ready to begin life anew.

Life imitates the constancy of the tide with the promise that nothing ever stays the same for very long. That's the one constant you can count on--that there will always be change. We resist change much of the time, welcome it in at other times. It's only in retrospect that we realize all change is good.

I love living in New England because I love the change of seasons. For me, they don't end or begin abruptly on Labor Day or Memorial Day. They gently fold into one another until almost without warning I become aware of the subtle differences around me. I feel it as the sun begins to sink low in the western sky earlier today. Everyone suddenly notices how early it gets dark and they all say, "Wow, how did that happen so quickly?"

I sit at a picnic table and begin to read from *The Call*, a book by one of my favorite authors, Oriah Mountain Dreamer. She is discussing her frustration over not being able to stay in touch with her inner self and her spirituality. One week she's right there, and a few weeks later she's totally out of touch with it, engulfed in the responsibilities and duties of life. I nod in agreement as I read, understanding exactly what she's talking about. We are hardest on ourselves when it comes to what we require and expect.

I begin to read an exquisite poem that she has quoted. The words are a reminder of God's love and forgiveness, for me and for everyone. I close the book and, with tears in my eyes, head toward the parking lot. I am aware of my whole body, every part of my being, as I stumble along the path from the beach to my car. I smell the fecund scent of the marsh whose tall grasses grow beside the path. I am reminded, all at once, of decades of being in this place as I feel broken apart by the words of the poem.

I am my smallest self in the midst of this sand and sky and ocean. As I begin to put the parts back together once again, I am still trying to stay in touch with the innermost part of me, and reside there a little longer this time. I have felt myself being torn apart, yet totally falling back into place again, broken and repaired in the same instant.

I know why I come here, just as I know there is something much, much greater than my small self. I am always reminded of it here, in a way that feels like a gentle hand on my head, smoothing back my hair and letting me know that everything will be alright.

I'LL HOLD YOU

Could I but hold you
'til the crimson light
of an early dawn
splashed through my window's view,
I'd calm your fears.

Could I but hold you
as the silver moon
on its nightly arc
climbed high through velvet skies,
I'd drink your tears.

Could I but see you
and then touch your face
I'd shape my smile to bring
you safe out of the dark
and heal your heart.

Could I but touch you,
and make your pain subside,
then a gift of peace
I'd pass from me to you
while we were one.

Chapter 37

"What you experience in your life is
your own creation. Therefore, you have the
power to change it any time you choose."
A Course in Miracles

Surviving the sorrows of my life has always been my
challenge. Just surviving is not enough though. There also
has to be a thriving and an implicit trust in the process
of life. Being patient with the unfolding of time after
spending hours walking with grief is important. Believing
in the goodness of life is imperative. You do not get the
joy without the sorrow. How could I have gotten through
the grievous and sorrowful times if I hadn't known, and
believed, that there would be joy when I climbed the next
hill? The challenge was in being resolute enough to make
the climb.

I cannot count the number of times I fell down while
climbing, sometimes flat on my face. There were so many
times when I wondered why these things had happened to
me, times when I wanted to scream, and beat my hands
on the table. There were times when I cried and yelled,
because someone I loved had been taken from me, by death
or distance. I didn't always accept it easily, or take it in my
stride. Yet, if I hadn't been able to summon up the will to
get up and try again, I would have missed the magnificent
view from the top of the next hill.

I had these thoughts as I sat on my dock and looked out over the lake I love so much. I know that to love and be loved is always worth the wait, and loss is still worth the price when you have loved and been loved. I cannot imagine giving up one minute of the joy that love brought to my life, just because of the sorrow that followed. Life is a treasure given to us, to live as we choose. In my opinion, there are only two choices, to live in the light or stay hidden in the darkness, in fear.

It's important to remember while struggling to figure out why some things happen, to simply let it go, and trust. Accepting what the future may bring and not having the need to figure it out frees us from the fear of loss or lack. Trauma makes us afraid and causes us to fear the process of life, but we all have the power within us to change that and not become a victim or the saboteur of our own happiness.

If my own perspective can change daily or even more often than that, how can anything be finite or permanent? I can sit in my canoe and write as it turns ever so slightly, when all the while it is simply bringing me back to my original position. It's the same with life. We come full circle as we live, and come home to ourselves in the end.

As I drove home the other day, I thought about something I had seen a few months before on a bumper sticker about not postponing joy. It seemed like it might be a good quote to put at the end of my book, and so I scribbled it on a little pad on the passenger seat of my car. Just then, as if to reinforce my thinking, a car passed me with a bumper sticker on the back that read, "DON'T POSTPONE JOY!"

So, I don't postpone joy. When something wakes me up in the early hours of the morning, before the sun comes up, I pay attention and get out of bed. I walk outside and view the broad expanse of sky over the lake. Each morning is different, each morning is unique and each morning displays a work of art that rivals the one before.

I sit on the steps with my camera near by, wanting to preserve the view and the feelings that the view evokes. My heart is wide-open as my breath catches in my throat. My eyes are hardly wide enough to take it in, so my other senses join my sight and register the glorious view before me and around me. Although the sky and the colors change from day to day, it is always amazingly beautiful to me, like the winter photo on the front cover. All the colors of the rainbow have taken their turn in surprising me as the seasons and the weather change.

This morning is no exception. I walk barefoot out to the steps on the landing. The air feels clean and crisp, as it does in the fall. The trees across the lake are just beginning to turn colors. I sit down, cozy in my big sweatshirt, and I turn my eyes up to the thunderclouds overhead. For a few moments they are shaded in pink and rose, along the eastern horizon, the magnificence of the colors reflected in the waters of the lake. But it's only a window in time and changes ever so quickly. The thin strip of blue and gold that heralded the arrival of the rising sun disappears behind the rolling dark clouds and obliterates the sun's rays.

Within minutes the colorful sky has disappeared. The breathtaking panorama that brings out such a reverence in me is gone. The thick puffy, gray clouds are darkening, saturated by the rain that is forecasted for the day. Ah, but I have had the privilege of peeking into that chink in time, a humbling experience. An imitation of life, it's a reminder of bright skies and love, of darkness and sorrow, and of the two traveling side by side on the journey.

FOR ALWAYS

Go my Love, and I will stay beside you,
into the darkness or out in to the light.
I will be there with you always.
I run the race...I walk the journey.
I plow through sludge.
I swim upstream.
I ride on your soul as it takes wing.
I fly with your heart
when it leaps from your chest.
And always, I'm beside you.

Walk on my Love, and I will keep the pace.
Hold tight to love, and know its worth.
Through night and day believe its truth.
I'm in the smile you smile,
the tears you cry,
the laugh that bursts from within you,
and even the frown that darkens your handsome face.
I live in the shiver that runs through your body
when boundless joy spills over.

So never doubt that I am with you always,
wherever that may be.
Look deep inside your heart
And you will surely find me there,
because now and forever your heart is my home...

DEATH IS NOTHING AT ALL

Death is nothing at all. I have only slipped away into the next room. I am I, and you are you. Whatever we were to each other, that we still are. Call me by my old familiar name speak to me in the easy way which you always used. Put no difference in your tone, wear no forced air of solemnity or sorrow. Laugh as we always laughed at the little jokes we enjoyed together. Play, smile, think of me, pray for me. Let my name be ever the household word that it always was, let it be spoken without effect, without the trace of a shadow on it. Life means all that it ever meant. It is the same as it ever was; there is unbroken continuity. Why should I be out of mind because I am out of sight? I am waiting for you, for an interval, somewhere very near, just around the corner. All is well.

Henry Scott Holland
1847-1918 Canon of St. Paul's Cathedral

369110